"I want to know Christ and the power of his resurrection and the fellowship of sharing in his sufferings, becoming like him in death...I press on to take hold of that for which Christ Jesus took hold of me." Philippians 3:10-12 (NIV)

The words of the Apostle Paul echo the deepest sentiments of many Christians. Ray Beeson further extrapolates: "If you *really* want to know Christ, you must truly see the cross for all that it is."

That I May Know Him sets forth the realities of the cross — both its legacy of suffering and its triumphant victory that gave us salvation and more: the gifts of sanctification, justification, redemption, atonement, forgiveness, the authority to teach and preach, and the power to cast out the devil! In these pages, the author clears up any confusion you may have about the subject of the cross and shows how at the beginning, middle, and end of the cross you will find God's love.

Through the examination of the patterns and examples of Christ's life, you will learn how to manifest His perfection in your own life to achieve, among many things:

- Maturity — mental, emotional, and spiritual
- Ministry — Christ's love — the heart of Christian service
- Obedience — surrendering rebellion

That I May Know Him will lead you to a place where your path will cross with Christ's so you can walk with Him, united forever.

That I May Know HIM

That I May Know HIM

RAY BEESON

Fleming H. Revell Company
Old Tappan, New Jersey

Unless otherwise identified, Scripture quotations in this book are from the Holy Bible, New International Version, copyright © 1973, 1978, 1984 International Bible Society. Used by permission of Zondervan Bible Publishers.

Scripture quotations identified KJV are from the King James Version of the Bible.

Library of Congress Cataloging-in-Publication Data
Beeson, Ray.
    That I may know him / Ray Beeson.
        p. cm.
    Includes bibliographical references.
    ISBN 0-8007-5338-0
    1. Jesus Christ—Biography—Meditations.   2. Christian
biography—Palestine—Meditations.   I. Title.
BT306.5.B44   1990
232.9'01—dc20   89–29671
[B]   CIP

Copyright © 1990 by Ray Beeson
Published by the Fleming H. Revell Company
Old Tappan, New Jersey 07675
Printed in the United States of America

TO
Ralyn, Rob, Amy, and Amanda

Contents

Acknowledgments

I feel humbled indeed to know a few of the wonderful truths of the cross of Jesus Christ. From the writings of many faithful servants of the Lord I have gleaned many of the valuable truths in this book. I thank God that they took the time and energy to record what they learned, since their work has been a good part of my inspiration.

I also wish to acknowledge two servants of the Lord whose lives have touched mine: my grandparents, Antone and Frieda Wymer, who are now with the Lord. When I was a child they faithfully guided me toward the things of the Lord. Their love and instruction in the Word carefully molded my life for eternity.

Finally, I owe so much to Lance Ralston and Dave Guzik for their help and guidance in writing this book.

Preface

Nothing in Scripture and nothing in life convinces me more than the cross of Jesus Christ that I should serve God with my whole heart. That God would suffer seems the greatest paradox in history, bearing little resemblance to anything rational. How could the Almighty God suffer? It makes no sense. It seems absurd and stands as one of the greatest monuments to foolish thinking. This suffering God, however, has caught my attention and arrested my rebellion. Because of the cross, human wisdom is exposed for its self-love and defamed for its arrogancy.

A Hindu was deeply moved by the cross. "If," he said, "the heart that rules the universe is like the gentle heart that broke on Calvary, he can have my heart forever." But until a person truly sees the cross for all it is, he will be tempted to say with Aldous Huxley, "I cannot see a shadow or tittle of evidence that God is love."

11

A number of years ago, I set out to find Christ—to *really* know him. Paul's words to the Philippians challenged me: "That I may know him . . ." (3:10 KJV). I do not mean to indicate that I was seeking salvation, for I had been assured of this grace for many years. But something deep within cried for a far more intimate fellowship than any surface acquaintance could offer.

I studied his life, wanting to know everything possible about him, both human and divine. I wanted to know more than the words he spoke; I wanted to know the manner and attitude in which he spoke them . . . to know not only his acts but his ways as well. The children of Israel knew his mighty works, but Moses knew his voice personally.

I have found much because there is so much to find, but the most inescapable discovery about Jesus has been his love. If we were to condense all Scripture into just a few succinct statements, we would find the first would be that God loves us, simply yet significantly. For all the theology contained therein, it boils down to God's wonderful love for mankind.

The second statement would concern the sum total of the commandments of God. All the laws and the prophets collectively condense into two commandments: "You shall love God with all your being and your neighbor as yourself."

I bear a great deal of shame in having to report that, for as much as I have put into my Christian experience, I have fallen far short of producing or of having had produced in me God's desired effect of love. The solution to any of our failures, however, is not to give up in discouragement but to go on seeking him. That is what I am doing. I would like to invite you to join me in seeking the Christ of the cross. May it be a wonderful experience for both of us, perhaps even a "magnificent journey."

Introduction

We have been called to follow Christ, to be conformed to his image. This is such an unfathomable task that it is easy to despair of the goal. Has the experience and perfection of Christ ever seemed so far away, so unattainable, that you have entertained the idea of throwing in the towel? Maybe you have stumbled and fallen over the same sin so many times that you've occasionally wondered if victory in Christ is for everyone else but you. Perhaps you have been tempted in a way that left you well shaken. Join the ranks, my friend. You are not alone!

Sometimes Christ's perfection seems so lofty that we lose hope of ever becoming like him. One moment our hearts burn with a holy passion to be pure, to be like him, to know him fully; the next moment we find ourselves frustrated and beaten.

The purpose of this book is to show the pattern and example of the life of Christ in relation to our own lives in order to see how he is available to help us overcome the struggles of life. We will identify aspects of his life that bear directly upon our own. The Holy Spirit wants to walk us through the experiences of Jesus in order to find *his* perfection. We have the glorious promise that "he who began a good work in you will carry it on to completion until the day of Christ Jesus."[1]

Within the life of Jesus are the answers to all the questions of our lives. In him all the mysteries of the universe are hidden. Everything mankind needs or desires is found through knowing Christ. But for all he possesses, it is amazing that so few of earth's inhabitants seek him. Perhaps this would be vastly different if only they knew him.

We are created so uniquely, so full of wonder, so beyond comprehension, that we constantly marvel at the complexities of our makeup. The truth is, we know very little about ourselves.

After centuries, the medical field still has a long way to go in understanding the human body. Although the advancements have been great, the surface has been barely scratched. We have probed the mind and emotions of the soul with psychology and have found an ocean that defies crossing. The human spirit is so difficult to perceive that it appears but a flickering light to our dull awareness.

Science continues to look for answers to life but examines only the architecture and not the Architect. This is like trying to study and understand the paintings of a great master without ever looking at the master himself. Science studies the facts of the material universe, but it is incapable of examining the intent and the reason behind what it sees. If man were merely concerned with what has taken place historically, he could forever be content with looking at physical cause and effect. His thirst could be quenched with mere knowledge. But simple facts only touch certain surface needs. They satisfy the curiosity of intellect but fail to answer the questions that arise from the longings of the soul.

Who are we? Why are we here? Where are we going? These are questions never to be answered by examining the creation. They must be answered by examining the Creator.

Mankind has always asked questions. Are we of any meaning to anyone or anything? Is there a reason for our existence? Why?

Why not? Many things operate and function satisfactorily without my understanding or even my approval. Maybe the universe is doing all right. Maybe creation is coming along fine. That sounds nice, but no one really believes it. Most of us believe that something is desperately wrong with this planet. Some may argue that the reason things seem so wrong in this world is that no one living in it is in his right mind. But that only further indicates that something is wrong. The fact that we label some things wrong is an indication there must be other things which are right. We would never be tempted to question or to ask why if things functioned correctly.

From newborn babies to wizened old men, human beings seem to agree on one thing: they disagree with the way things are. We want more out of life. We want a better world. We want things to be different. But try as we might, we usually fail to find the good we believe exists somewhere.

Moral righteousness, which is practiced to some degree everywhere on earth, suggests that a "normal rightness" does in fact exist. The man who wants to get better in some area of his life is acknowledging that there is a higher standard. But what is this higher standard?

When people argue, it is often over the claim that one is right while the other is wrong. Such dissension gives us reason to believe in some kind of universal value system. Each one is claiming to know what proper values are while insisting the other does not.

The world over, people find themselves involved in conflicts over moral and ethical beliefs. Our arguments proceed out of a desire to adhere to a common set of values only vaguely comprehended yet believed to be a standard for all men. Something intuitively centered deep within us tries to line up on a uniform yet blurry target. The great challenge in life is to find that standard, to know what is universally right for every man, to come to clear vision, to hit the bull's-eye.

This is where God comes in. But who is God? Can he really be known? What purpose does he have for his creation? And why is he so silent? A. W. Tozer realized that man was light-years away in his understanding of God:

> To most people God is an inference, not a reality. He is a deduction from evidence which they consider adequate, but He remains personally unknown to the individual. "He *must* be," they say, "therefore we believe He is." Others do not go even so far as this; they know Him only by hearsay. They have never bothered to think the matter out for themselves, but have heard about Him from others, and have put belief in him into the back of their minds along with various odds and ends that make up their total creed. To many others, God is but an ideal, another name for goodness, or beauty, or truth; or He is law, or life, or the creative impulse back of the phenomena of existence.[2]

We would like to reach into heaven to bring him down to earth, but we cannot. We engage in searching for him within our souls in hopes of finding him there, but we do not. The age-old quest of man has been to find God and the values under which we should live.

For many, the search continues. For some, however, it has ended. Some have found religion. Some are satisfied with the god of self. Others are content to serve a devil. Still others have found Jesus the expressed image of God.

Jesus, the founder of a unique life-style often called Christianity? Jesus, who owns television stations and satellites? The Jesus who raises finances and promises luxury to his followers? The Jesus who gets angry easily and gives out long lists of do's and don'ts?

No! Not *that* Jesus. Instead, the Jesus who was born in Bethlehem, the one who walked the streets of Jerusalem, who prayed in Gethsemane, went to Calvary, rose from the dead, the one who is coming to earth again, *the one who is God*. This is the one the Father is most interested in revealing to humanity.

If you have ever wondered if God really cares about you, if you have ever asked why there are suffering and sorrows in this life, then you will want to examine carefully the life of Christ while he was here on earth. You will want to discover everything possible about his earthly existence. In doing so, you will find the answers and solutions to the many questions and problems that plague us.

To understand this Man called Jesus, let us follow him briefly through that wondrous moment of his birth, through his time of growth, and on into his ministry. Then let us go with him to Gethsemane, from there to Calvary, and past that to the Resurrection. Finally, let us look with him into eternity.

No doubt there will be some who, as they read this book, are not certain who Jesus Christ is. If you are one of these people, let me share with you in this book what the Scriptures say about him. Throughout the text you will find reference to hundreds of Scriptures that will help you understand what the Bible says about the most unique Man in history.

That I May Know HIM

1
The Birth of Jesus Christ

A rainbow cannot truly convey the grace, majesty, and character of the person who made it. Nor can a snowcapped mountain, a sunset, or the thunderous surf of the beach. People may mean well when they say they find God in these things, but they really only fool themselves. For although each testifies of his reality and greatness, not one of them reveals what man's heart longs to hear. None of these images satisfies the desire to know God's true personality and experience his love. All of these aspects of creation, as marvelous as they are, fall far short of adequately telling man how God really feels about him. *The vacuum of the human heart can never be filled with the beauty and grandeur of the universe. It must be filled with God.*

John MacBeath wrote:

> Beauty is an abstraction until it finds expression in a flower. Music is a fantasy until the notes of an instrument give it speech. Art is ethereal until it embodies itself in sculpture or in picture. The great things of created and uncreated thought are only grasped and understood when they find expression in some easy, intelligible, and often substantial form.[1]

But for all the form seems to say about the artist, it is little more than his signature and conveys but a tiny aspect of his character. The divine art gallery of creation shows us where he has been but tells only a little about him.

Christ, the Scriptures tell us, was to be God's revelation of himself to mankind in a way man could comprehend. Creation says, "God is." Jesus says, "I Am." Creation is the form and substance of his handiwork. Jesus is the heart and soul. Oh, yes, God can still be seen in a baby's smile and sensed in the solitude of a majestic forest, but the child lying in the manger was, according to Scripture, the first tangible expression of God himself. No longer was he a voice out of the heavens. Suddenly there was person and personality which could be seen and touched. And he could touch in return.

Although the heavens declare the glory of God, causing men who do not worship him to be "without excuse,"[2] it was necessary for the impersonal to become personal, for the ethereal to become tangible. We know that "since the creation of the world God's invisible qualities . . . have been clearly seen . . ."[3] yet man would never know God's true love and his desire for intimacy with humanity without a clear expression of his personality. But who would ever guess that that expression would make its first appearance in a dingy stable among smelly animals? God was the great unknown whom Jesus came to make known.

God's intention was to help man redevelop an intimate relationship with himself and in the process discover and embrace the lost standard of living. For man to do this, however, he would have to turn around and go in another direction. He would have to repent, and he would need to be set free from bondage to Satan. But because of his vile condition as well as his slavery to the Enemy, man has always failed to change direction and become the completed person he needs to be. As C. S. Lewis said, there is a catch: "Only a bad person needs to repent: only a good person can repent perfectly. The worse you are the more you need it and the less you can do it. The only person who could do it perfectly would be a perfect person—and he would not need it."[4] And so God decided to help us to surrender, yield, submit, and die in one area; and to stand, fight, and resist in another.

But for all the things that God would need to do to help man, most were outside his character. In a sense, they were impossible for him to do. God does not need to surrender, yield, resist, or die to self. To lend part of himself to us in order to help us, there would have to be the same qualities in him that needed to be manifest in us. In order to help us surrender, there would have to be some experience where he had surrendered. To help an individual die to self, he would have to undergo a similar experience of dying to himself.

But none of these experiences were ever his. However, if God were to become a man, if he were to practice obedience, and especially if he were to die, then he would be able to give us the aid we need. He could share his experiences with us. If he were to suffer as we do, then the impartation of himself into our lives would contain the ingredients necessary for assisting us in being different. We needed to change. Something had gone wrong and needed to be made right. But we needed help in order to change. And Jesus was about to make that provision.

The Prophets Tell of His Coming

Long before he was found by kings, shepherds, and wise men, the birth of Jesus was foretold in Scripture: "The virgin will be with child and will give birth to a son, and will call him Immanuel."[5] Immanuel! Could it really be that God himself planned to set foot among men? Could it be that mankind would someday experience "God with us"?[6]

John the Baptist had been sent by God to bear witness of the coming Messiah, the Christ. He did this faithfully. Perhaps because of persecution and because Jesus failed, in John's eyes, to show the qualifications of a conquering king, he began to doubt and question. While John was in prison he sent his disciples to ask Jesus, "Are you the one who was to come, or should we expect someone else?"[7]

Men had long believed that God would someday send them a Savior. The Old Testament prophets had made it clear that God was going to send One among them who would be more than an ordinary man. But was Jesus this person? Could he really throw off Roman tyranny? Could he restore the culture and the economy? Could he keep the nation safe from invasion? Could he sit in the seat of a king? The Jews of that era never questioned the prophecy of a coming king. It was Jesus they questioned.

Jeremiah had written, " 'The days are coming,' declares the Lord, 'when I will raise up to David a righteous Branch, a King who will reign wisely and do what is just and right in the land. In his days Judah will be saved and Israel will live in safety.' "[8] It is easy to see why so many questioned him in the beginning. If this Jesus was that King who was to come, he surely had a strange way of setting up his kingdom.

But Christ was not concerned about a present external kingdom for himself and therefore was not concerned with that kind of acceptance. He was in the process of establishing mankind into an eternal kingdom. He had journeyed to earth for that purpose. Even as he walked slowly among the people, Christ was moving quickly to complete the plan for man's salvation, a plan developed from the foundation of the world. Shortly he would be able to say, "It is finished."[9]

His Unique Entrance

During the reign of Herod the Great, there lived in Nazareth a man and woman whose names were Joseph and Mary. Both were godly people who had pledged themselves to each other in marriage. As was the custom among the Jews, they were to give themselves to a time of waiting before the marriage was actually consummated. It was during this time that Joseph discovered Mary was already pregnant. Shocked at what he felt was a betrayal of his trust, he believed his only choice was to privately divorce her for her supposed infidelity.

But Mary had not been unfaithful. She had been chosen by God to fulfill his plan for bringing a Savior into the world. Some time before, the angel Gabriel had come and proclaimed to her what was about to happen. He told her that the Holy Spirit would come upon her, the power of the Most High would overshadow her, and the one to be born would be called the Son of God.

Then it was Joseph's turn. The angel appeared to him in a dream and said, "Do not be afraid to take Mary home as your wife, because what is conceived in her is from the Holy Spirit.

She will give birth to a son, and you are to give him the name Jesus, because he will save his people from their sins."[10]

Mankind, far from the intended purpose for which God had made him, needed to be rescued, and God was determined to be involved. But he was not going to do it directly in his capacity of God in heaven. His plan was to live among us, taste our pain, and rescue us—as a human being.

And so it happened one star-filled night that Jesus was born in a manger in Bethlehem.

His Sinless Nature

God's plan was for Jesus to be born like the rest of us. But if he were born through normal conception, the very thing that causes man's problems would be passed on to him through birth. The very nature of sin, originating in Adam, that is passed from parent to offspring and makes us Satan's slaves, would bring him into the same bondage. It would also make him incapable of rescuing a lost world. One prisoner cannot free another; only one outside the bondage of sin could set us free. Only a virgin birth would produce a human being over whom the Enemy would have no control: a sinless human being.

Sin is not only personally damaging to one's life; it is also what gives Satan access to an individual. Since Satan had no rights in the life of Jesus because he was sinless, Jesus was free to function as Adam did before he fell. This new, unbridled power on earth gave Satan his first real cause for concern. He had operated with almost total immunity since the time he took control of the planet from Adam. Now, everything he had gained was at stake. This second "Adam," in perfect relationship with his Father, could begin to put an end to Satan's entire kingdom.

Fear, no doubt, surged through demon ranks as consideration was given to what would happen with the advent of a sinless human being. Devils scurried to attempt his destruction. But neither demons nor death have power over sinlessness. The only plan that would have even a slight chance was one that would cause Jesus to disobey the Father. Disobedience would render him as ineffective as the first Adam, and humanity would lose all hope of ever being saved.

As long as Jesus remained in harmony with the Father, his humanity could be anointed by the Holy Spirit, and eventually Satan would be conquered. The first Adam would never have lost out to the Enemy if he had remained in fellowship with God. Once Adam's intimacy with God was broken, no power remained within him to resist the Enemy, and mankind was soon trapped in satanic slavery.

The God-Man

Initially man had difficulty believing that Jesus was God. The Pharisees, especially, challenged the idea. Later, the problem was not believing that he was God; it was believing that he was man. In fact, one of the first errors the Church had to address concerning Christ was an attack on his humanity. In the earliest days of the faith, a group called the Docetists, part of a larger group called Gnostics, or knowing ones, said that Jesus only "seemed" to be a man. They found it impossible to believe that God's love would be strong enough to cause him to come as a fellow human being to share our experiences.

In order to save humanity, God planned to impart himself "totally" into a human frame. Jesus was not part God—he was completely God. His earthly body was completely man. He became flesh and blood like all other men, and by doing so would be able to accomplish a wonderfully unique plan.

First, he would establish a new rulership in the midst of the one that was presently governing because of Adam's default. God never gave this planet to Satan. Satan acquired its rulership from Adam only after Adam, in a state of disobedience, gave it to him.

Jesus could establish this new kingdom because he was not part of the old kingdom and because there was nothing within or around him to prevent such an endeavor. Sin in us prevents us from challenging the Enemy.

Second, God would prove his undying love for lost humanity by leaving the security of heaven and placing himself where he would face pain. He was saying in essence, "I love you enough to come to where you are in order to get you back."

Leaving the splendor of the celestial realm also meant that Jesus would place himself at risk in order to complete his rescue mission. *Without the possibility of failure there would have been no real temptation, no real pain, and therefore no real victory.* His suffering and sorrow proved beyond question his incredible love for humanity.

To truly understand Jesus, we must first see him in the form of God and second in the likeness of men, not as both God and man but as the God-man. This means that deity and humanity now dwell together in one person. Being truly man, he did not relinquish his nature as God. One did not replace the other. But in order to complete his mission, he put aside his glory to take on the nature of a servant. He simply limited his power during "the days of his flesh."[11] In order to truly humble himself, he let go of his heavenly position of authority. His glory did not cease to exist but was now neither used by him nor seen by men.

Imagine that a great king, desiring to help his subjects, disguises himself and lives among the poor and needy. He dresses in humble clothes and walks in the slums of the city. He sleeps in the shambles of an old tenant house and eats meagerly on the few dollars he occasionally is able to earn. He doesn't just watch the people; he lives with them until he feels their pain. Now it is true that he is living in unfamiliar surroundings and is dressed unlike royalty, but does this make him any less a king? Though he is still the same royal person and still holds the same authority that has always been his, it is difficult to use it and accomplish his mission at the same time. It is not until he is recognized that men will respond to his authority. And then they will only recognize him hesitantly until he is once again placed upon his throne. But when he finally arrives, the people to whom he came will love him more for what he tried to do in order to help them.

It is this marvelous aspect of love on the part of Jesus that endears him to us today. How strangely humbled is the human heart upon recognizing such great sacrifice.

The Preexistent God

Most who deny the biblical Jesus do so by assaulting his deity. There are few today who will challenge the affirmation that Christ was a man who once lived on earth. There is simply too much evidence from historical writing to challenge his existence as a man. Historians such as Flavius Josephus mentioned him in their writings. But that he is God manifest in human flesh fosters another kind of debate. The Scriptures, however, affirm his deity. The writer of Hebrews recognized that the universe was created through Jesus (*see* Hebrews 1:1, 2). When writing to the Ephesians, the Apostle Paul noted the same thing (*see* Ephesians 3:9).

To some people, the fact that Christ created everything does not prove his deity. Their argument is that as a creation of God, he was then sent forth to create. But the Prophet Nehemiah silences that debate when he records a Levitical praise offering establishing the Lord God as the Creator of the universe: "You alone are the Lord. You made the heavens, even the highest heavens, and all their starry host, the earth and all that is on it, the seas and all that is in them. You give life to everything, and the multitudes of heaven worship you."[12] If the children of Israel proclaimed God the Creator and Paul claimed Jesus was the Creator (Colossians 1:15–17), then if Scripture is held as the Word of God, the only logical conclusion is that Jesus is God. He is not the creation of God. He is God the Creator.

Christ himself openly proclaimed his deity: "Jesus said to them, 'My Father is always at his work to this very day, and I, too, am working.' For this reason the Jews tried all the harder to kill him; not only was he breaking the Sabbath, but he was even calling God his own Father, making himself equal with God."[13] The religious Jews of that day believed humanity was so sinful that God and man could not be identified together. For Jesus to assert that God was his Father was to them a statement in which he was declaring himself God. It angered them to think this person whom they plainly recognized as one of their own people would make such a statement.

Jesus was seen as an ordinary man, at least until his ministry began. But even then the Jewish leaders refused to acknowledge his miracles as a sign from heaven. Hardened through their own religious pride, they could not see that "the Son is the radiance of God's glory and the *exact* representation of his being, sustaining all things by his powerful word."[14]

Some people have a difficult time appreciating the reality of

God. For many, there is the problem of comprehending the concept of three persons in One Being without coming up with three gods. But God is not asking us to fathom his composition. He is asking us to accept Jesus.

To estimate God, to grasp his being, to understand his fashioning is ludicrous for finite man and especially for finite "fallen" man. So if God appears to be three—Father, Son, and Holy Spirit—yet says he is one, who is man that he should question? Who is he that he should demand to understand? We have not yet begun to grasp the wonders of creation. Should we dare claim to comprehend God? Some, however, set about to proclaim what we as yet cannot understand, and they do so as if it had been made very clear. They endeavor to explain how God is put together. The simple truth is that we are left with a mystery concerning the makeup of God. Yet God has left no mystery to the fact that Jesus is not only the Son of God, he is also God the Son.

2
A New Birth for Mankind

When Jesus responded to Nicodemus' inquiry about new life by saying, "You must be born again,"[1] the man was puzzled. How could a person be born a second time? How could a man be completely rebuilt, made new to the last detail? Christ was going to explain how, and Nicodemus was about to discover more than just a new chance in life. He was about to discover life itself!

The New Birth Foretold

Jesus revealed to Nicodemus that man needed a radical transformation.

What God promised to do to the Jewish people through the Prophet Ezekiel when he prophesied, "I will sprinkle clean water on you, and you will be clean; I will cleanse you from all

your impurities and from all your idols. I will give you a new
heart and put a new spirit in you; I will remove from you your
heart of stone and give you a heart of flesh. And I will put my
Spirit in you and move you to follow my decrees and be
careful to keep my laws,"[2] he was about to do for all mankind
through Jesus Christ. As the birth of Jesus had been foretold,
so the new birth of humanity had been promised. The Jewish
prophets had confirmed that God would one day make a new
covenant with mankind—one in which he would give them a
new life, a new heart, and a new start.

Paul the Apostle noted that this tremendous change was
available through Christ: "Therefore, if anyone is in Christ,
he is a new creation; the old has gone, the new has come!"[3]

God had set about to rescue lost humanity. He had come to
save something very precious to himself. If man would but
listen to him and then follow him, he could be freed from the
darkness and emptiness of self-absorption. No prison cell can
hold a man in more bondage than his own sinful self. But
Christ has come in power to thrust open prison doors.

Regeneration

Receiving spiritual life in God through Christ brings significant change. The oldness of the life separated from God is
replaced by a complete newness. Everything changes—goals,
motives, perceptions, ambitions, relationships.

Although most people hate their present condition, they are
still reluctant to accept a new and better way. Why? Because
of the blindness of the human heart. This lack of perception,
inherited from our forefathers, is further reinforced by the god
of this age. Unless our eyes are somehow opened, we refuse
to believe God's offer is anything better than what we already
have. This blindness is partially and temporarily removed

when the Holy Spirit convicts us of our "lost condition." It is completely removed, however, only when we accept Christ and commit our lives fully to him.

God says we must be holy, but we are incapable of attaining such a state. The more we try, the greater our despair. Our only hope is to have another nature, a holy one, imparted to us.

Sometimes, when one performs the works of Christian living, he is referred to as having been converted. But acting like a Christian does not indicate a real regeneration. True conversion means turning entirely to God and allowing him to enter our very being. It is an event that encompasses the whole of life.

But turning *to* God means turning *away from* sin and self. The "turning from" is the act of repentance. Repentance means to change one's mind with a corresponding change in behavior. A person may go to church, pay tithes, and practice honesty in every detail of life without having repented and without the benefit of regeneration. By contrast, regeneration does not give God something, but he gives us something. He has given us himself and we have received him. Our reception of him reconciles us to God.

The Uniqueness of the New Birth

Just as Christ's entrance into the world was unique, so is the new birth of the child of God. Again, regeneration, with its corresponding reconciliation, comes only one way: through the person and work of Jesus Christ. He said, "I am the way and the truth and the life. No one comes to the Father except through me."[4] The Apostle Peter stood before the rulers of Israel and proclaimed of Jesus, "Salvation is found in no one else, for there is no other name under heaven given to men by which we must be saved."[5] It is just that simple and easy.

But is there only one way? Shouldn't there be other possibilities? Doesn't the Bible say God is not willing that any should perish? If God really wants all to come to repentance and escape spiritual and eternal death, why doesn't he broaden the way or provide many ways? The amazing thing is not that God hasn't provided *more* ways to new life but that he has provided any at all.

Man's basic problem is rebellion. If God had offered five ways to reconciliation, we would want ten. Man's rebellion is not against the method of salvation; it is against God himself. Because God is rejected, his method is rejected as well. Paul the Apostle shares the extent of this rebellion with the Romans: "For although they knew God, they neither glorified him as God nor gave thanks to him, but their thinking became futile and their foolish hearts were darkened."[6] Jesus, when sharing God's love for humanity, noted that "light has come into the world, but men loved darkness instead of light because their deeds were evil."[7]

Thus, in reality, coming to new birth and new life is accomplished by laying down personal rebellion against God and accepting his Life.

Our New Nature

E. Y. Mullins wrote:

> A redeemed drunkard, with vivid memory of past hopeless struggles and a new sense of power through Christ, was replying to the charge that "his religion was a delusion." He said: Thank God for the delusion; it put clothes on my children and shoes on their feet and bread

in their mouths. It has made a man of me and it has put
joy and peace in my home, which had been a hell. If this
is a delusion, may God send it to the slave of drink
everywhere, for their slavery is an awful reality.[8]

When we experience the new birth, we receive a new nature, and that new nature rejects sin and prompts acts of
righteousness. It reacts against the "presence" of sin because
of the holy presence of Christ in the life.

Sin also loses its "power." Because of Christ's power in the
life, the force of sin is gone, and "sin shall not be your
master."[9] Furthermore, God cancels sin's "penalty." Because
of the righteous presence of Christ in the life, God looks at us
and sees the life and righteousness of his Son in residence.
Thus he regards us as righteous—in right standing with him.

Delivered from the *penalty* of sin, we are released from fear
and guilt. Delivered from the *power* of sin, we enjoy freedom
and potential growth in Christlikeness. Delivered from the
presence of sin, we gain confidence and boldness in our relationship with God.

Grace Offered to the Rebellious

"Justice" is getting what we deserve.
"Mercy" is not getting what we deserve.
"Grace" is getting better than we deserve.
But how do we know what we deserve?
We tend to assume that we deserve God's blessing, and
that we are good and merit his favor. But if in fact we do not,
then how would we know anything was wrong unless that
which is right was disclosed? Before God could effect his
rescue mission by the use of the cross, he first had to show us
that there was a problem. This, no doubt, is why Calvary
stands thousands of years beyond the first sin.

The Old Testament gives us a measuring stick for righteousness. It proves not only that man is wrong but that he is unable to become right.

To show us the extent of our depravity, God began revealing himself to mankind. That revelation allowed us to see the great gulf between him and us. When he said he was holy, righteous, just, kind, or merciful, these were not statements just to glorify himself. They were statements that would allow us to compare ourselves with the Ideal. But each revelation only showed us how far away we really were.

As God spoke, men learned his character. All they had before was their superstitions about the spirit world—incredible deceptions by the Enemy of man's soul. They could not "trust" God because he had never really been revealed as one who could be trusted. He was not a shield, a provider, a healer, or any of the things we understand him to be today, until he came to man with those announcements. When the Children of Israel reached Canaan, the promised land, they understood far more about God than they did when they were in slavery in Egypt.

The Old Testament, then, shows us that we need God's grace and mercy. The New Testament shows us that we have it in Jesus Christ. The Old Testament tells us who we are. The New Testament shows us what we can become. In the Old, Noah is a drunkard. In the New, he is a man of righteousness. In the Old, Abraham is a liar. In the New, he is a man of faith. In the Old, Moses is a murderer. In the New, he is God's deliverer. In the Old, David is both adulterer and murderer. In the New, he is a man after God's own heart.

If God had not allowed us to see our own destructive capabilities, we would never have seen our need for a Savior. If God had saved Adam immediately after the Fall, Adam never would have fully known, as we do today, of the destructive nature of rebellion.

During the Old Testament era, God watched man fumble along in his waywardness. Any divine intrusion was met by resistance. So blinded and rebellious through sin is the soul of man that the slightest touch of God upon his domain results in violent reaction. The Pharaoh of Moses' day is typical. All God had to do was touch his sensitivity to self-pleasing and he became a madman. When asked to let God's people go from slavery, he rejected the proposal out of fear of losing some comfort. His selfishness was so powerful that it eventually cost the lives of thousands of his people, including his own son.

Throughout the Old Testament, God has shown us our dilemma with sin. Throughout the New Testament, he has shown us our hope through the grace which is found in Christ.

Now he stands to welcome the repentant sinner: "Here I am! I stand at the door and knock. If anyone hears my voice and opens the door, I will come in and eat with him, and he with me."[10] But not all believe. Many find it difficult to believe that God's grace is sufficient to touch their sinful lives. John Bunyan, author of *Pilgrim's Progress*, was such a person. How could God open his heart so wide as to take in such a foulmouthed sinner? Yet God's marvelous grace reached him through John 6:37: "Him that cometh to me I will in no wise cast out" (KJV).

Salvation Only in Jesus Christ

Have you truly been born again? Have you, as an act of your will, invited the Spirit of God to take up residence in you through Jesus Christ? Or are you counting on your endeavors to be a good person as your basis for God allowing you into his

holy heaven? Is it only a "religious" way of life among social
Christians with a once-a-week trip to church that occupies
your interest? Do you see your relationship with God based on
your ability to perform, or the church you attend, or is it as it
should be—based on a personal relationship with Jesus?

The Scripture says salvation is found only in Jesus Christ
and is evidenced by his Spirit living within. Only a personal
commitment to him, deepened by intimate communion
through his Word, prayer, and fellowship with other Christians, will guarantee a person eternal life.

3
The Growth of Jesus Christ

Human in Every Way

Is it possible to comprehend God in human flesh? What would a person be like who had no sin? Would there be anything noticeably different about him as he walked the streets, dined among friends, or sat in the synagogue?

Christ certainly was unique. But how was he different?

His appearance was not as dissimilar as one might think. He was as human as any other man, and his looks were not out of the ordinary. He was neither very good nor very bad looking. That he was God was not obvious because he had laid aside his glory. While in a human body he would not manifest his attributes as Almighty God.

For all that everyone else knew, Jesus was born the son of Joseph and Mary. Joseph, however, knew that Jesus was not from the seed of his own body. But he also knew that Mary had not been unfaithful to her marriage vows. This tiny baby was of God. Perhaps Joseph wrestled often with the concept, but he could not wrestle with the Word of God and so became the child's earthly guardian. But who could comprehend such a thing? Who was capable of looking at pudgy little cheeks and tiny fingers and whispering "Baby God?" Could Mary really understand that it was God she was holding in her arms? Did she ever say to herself as she looked at her clothesline, "Those are God's pajamas?"

He lay in the manger as completely human as any other person born on this planet. He cried when he was hungry and laughed when he was tickled. Mary and Joseph, no doubt, recognized that he was different. He did not have the same selfish, antagonistic, and rebellious characteristics as other children. In his early years, his community would see him simply as a good kid, but Mary knew there was more to him than simple decency or basic goodness.

As the years progressed, he grew in wisdom, stature, and favor with God and man. New information was added daily to his earthly knowledge. His body grew, inch by inch and pound by pound. He was highly thought of by those who knew him and regarded with admiration and respect.

He did not seek popularity by attempting to make a favorable impression on people, nor did he avoid acknowledgment of himself as a means of establishing a religious sanctity while wrapping himself in a mysterious veil of piety. He mixed with common people, entering into the ordinary relationships of everyday life. His holy life could never be confused with a hermit's life. All of the legitimate and healthy joys of living were his as much as anyone's. His clean, strong zest for life allowed innocent laughter and good fun without solemn face and starchy appearance.

People appreciated his straightforward uprightness. Prudishness, isolationism, condemnation, and criticism—trademarks of some religious individuals and their institutions—were never a part of the way in which Jesus dealt with others. Bitter critics sought to defame him for his lack of established religious propriety. Bending low and touching soiled lives, however, was not a part of their moral composition.

Jesus Learned to Do Physical Work

Joseph was a carpenter. He no doubt wanted his sons, including Jesus, to follow in his footsteps. He was to learn to cut, split, shave, and carve the wood into its desired form. That he had made everything that exists, including the wood he now handled, was not his present concern. He was learning, like everyone else.

Although Jesus' spirituality exceeded that of all other men, he was not beyond laboring with his hands. Nothing in him suggested that he was to rise above physical work.

Jesus Learned Obedience

Because of his sinless nature, Jesus' spirit was open to his heavenly Father. This became evident at a very young age. The Father had begun to impart to him wisdom from above. How amazing it is that Jesus the Creator became so completely human he needed to be instructed. He was willing to do this in order to effect a grand plan for the salvation of mankind.

Since from the beginning God's plan for the human race included the family and, in that arrangement, required that children be obedient to their parents, Jesus too was obligated. Luke records that even in the midst of doing the Father's specific will, he understood his obligation for obedience to his earthly parents: "Then he went down to Nazareth with them and was obedient to them."[1]

The key to the success of the mission Jesus was sent to perform lay in his willingness to be obedient to the Father in heaven. Any failure in this regard would open the door to sin; salvation for humanity would be doomed. Notice his readiness for compliance with the Father's will: "For I did not speak of my own accord, but the Father who sent me commanded me what to say and how to say it. I know that his command leads to eternal life. So whatever I say is just what the Father has told me to say."[2]

Obedience in Suffering

Perhaps what is most incomprehensible surrounding the advent of Jesus onto the human scene is that he would be forced to suffer like all other men in order to complete his mission: "Although he was a son, he learned obedience from what he suffered."[3] "For we do not have a high priest who is unable to sympathize with our weaknesses, but we have one who has been tempted in every way, just as we are—yet was without sin."[4]

For thirty-three years he faced suffering from the curse that affects all of us. Wind, rain, thirst, hunger, vile men, cursing, complaining and bitterness, the sight of sickness and disease, and the scenes of sorrow were all there to bring pain of one kind or another into his life. For man to suffer seems hardly reasonable, at least to the natural mind, but for God to do so defies human comprehension. Wonder and majesty on the one hand, and such diabolical pain on the other, are so inconsistent and contradictory that even in his grandest imagination man is incapable of putting them together. But the amazing thing that draws us to God is that they came together so we might be saved.

Some people are afraid of the humanity of Jesus. Since he

was without sin, they seem to want to put him in a glass case to guard against human defilement. Perhaps they want to protect his holy eyes from sin. They preach against sin not so much that others might be freed, but because God must not see sin and become angry. It is as though they feel some personal responsibility for making the world right outside of God's help. This kind of motivation springs from fear and not from love. All such theology prevents us from identifying with Jesus and leaves him as a Savior who never truly touches us.

But Jesus was human. He was tempted, he felt pain, and he knew sorrow. He did not hide among the trees so that kids throwing rocks would not influence him. He did not give 100 percent of his waking hours to praying and reading Scripture. He did not stand on the street corner telling people to repent or perish. Instead, he walked among men and women, often the vilest ones. He ate with publicans and sinners. He was not afraid to associate with tax collectors and prostitutes. He did not participate in their sin; nor did he condone it. He simply walked among them because there was no other way to tell them of God's love.

4
Christian Growth

Physical Growth

Some people who talk about following Christ do not consider the fact that we need to follow him with regard to our physical bodies. For some, to give any heed to the body is to feed carnal interests. Although our highest ideal should be the full functioning of our spirit, we will never accomplish that goal if the body is neglected. Good food, proper rest, sufficient exercise, and adequate relaxation all contribute greatly to our total well-being. The body is the temple of the Holy Spirit for believers in Christ. It needs proper care.

Since food is the fuel which runs the body, it is important that proper nutrition be maintained. Rest is also extremely important. A fast pace in life might get a lot of things done, but it might also wear out our bodies. The Sabbath of the Old Testament is not an archaic idea lost forever when the Law was fulfilled in Christ. Its principle is just as important as it ever was. It gives the body the opportunity to slow down long enough to rebuild what was torn down in six other days.

Exercise and relaxation also must not be neglected if we are to maintain good physical health. Whenever proper care of the body is overlooked, we subject ourselves to mental and spiritual difficulties.

Mental and Emotional Growth

The soul of man primarily encompasses the will, mind, and emotions. Most of what transpires in this realm is directly related to thought. Almost all of the "warfare" of life (the difficulties we face that cause depression, fear, worry, anxiety, false guilt, and discouragement) is waged in this arena.

We must never assume that because God promises to take care of us, we are free from obligation to do warfare ourselves, especially in the realm of the mind. The mind is one of the most extensively fought-upon battlefields in existence. We must guard our minds tenaciously. In Christ we have the right and ability to cast out evil thoughts and to bring into captivity unrighteous thoughts that try to crowd themselves into our minds.

Following Christ involves our body, soul, and spirit. Just as Jesus grew physically and mentally, so we are challenged to grow in all areas of our being. We must put on the whole armor of God—an active, continuous practice. And we are furthermore told to resist the Enemy—active behavior on the part of all Christians.

Fighting effectively involves yielding to Christ. This does not mean submitting passively or mindlessly to his control; it means willing cooperation, realizing that he can help us make the best decisions. Christ does not want to control us. He wants us to be in control of ourselves. But that is a condition that is possible only with his help.

If we had met the Lord on the shores of Galilee and he had said to us, "Follow me," we may have had little difficulty. To physically get up and go with him from one place to another would have been rather simple. But when the "Follow me" becomes a life call and means more than moving our bodies from one place to another, it takes on quite a different meaning. When it means we are no longer to walk in self-indulgence, when we are urged to fight in an incredible spiritual war, when we are asked to be ready to die, then "Follow me" means a great deal more. At this point the human will cries out, questioning and even rebelling.

The great battle is not in accomplishing Christ's tasks but in yielding to his call. The advent of Christ into the life of an individual is not a question of reason but one of surrender.

Stubbornness, rebellion, neglect, and procrastination become our worst enemies in giving Christ complete access to our lives.

It does not take long in serving him to find that we are, in our own strength, incapable of obeying his commands. We come quickly and abruptly to the end of self-sufficiency. And that is precisely where Jesus wants us to be. Only when we are totally destitute in our own abilities can he impart his Spirit unto us.

Failure in serving the Lord is almost always based on the fact that we have not received from Christ. From the moment we are saved we tend to emphasize how much we should be doing for God. On the contrary, we will never perform a single good deed or accomplish anything pleasing to God without first having sat long enough in his presence for the attributes of his character to become our own.

John MacBeath wrote:

Before the beginning of the Christian era profound minds
like Plato felt that man was made by nature to be intimate with God. But Jesus revealed a move from the
other side. He expressed God's great desire to be intimate with man, to enter into the life of man and trans-
form his world from within. . . . There is no remoteness
in God. He loves and enjoys the world down to the last
rose of summer or the last swallow in flight, and above
all, He loves and enjoys the nature of man.[1]

Receiving the Spirit of the Lord is not a one-time experience. It is a refreshment to be daily imparted to and appropriated by the believer. It is as unique as the wind and as
wonderful as a gentle spring rain.

Our problems go much deeper than our inability to follow
Jesus. They center on our very being and are spelled out in
pride, selfishness, jealousy, hatred, laziness, and scores of
other negative and hurtful character traits needing his precise
surgical hand in order to be removed. But it is not a matter of
concentrating on our unworthiness. It is a matter of submitting to divine surgery and to receiving care from the Great
Physician.

None of us want to be sick, or poor, or sad. We frequently
do not want to talk about our troubles and often do not want
to admit that we are in need. Only when we have been driven
to Jesus do we realize how desperately we need him.

When we were new believers, we enjoyed a wonderful love
relationship with Christ. But it dissipated ever so gradually for
many of us—often because of the cares of life. Sadly, we did
not even perceive that the love was gone. But in spite of our
condition, he still waits and longs for our fellowship.

Spiritual Growth

The spirit of man was made for fellowship with God and is
unfulfilled without him. *The vacuum in the human heart must be*

*filled with God through Jesus Christ. Nothing else satisfies man's
inner longing.*

Christ is the only "Reality"; not experiences, not accomplishments, and not even eternity can take his place. Certainly no demon will give lasting peace.

Many of us do not want to disobey him, but we do not love him enough to obey him completely, either. The Apostle Paul was so overwhelmed by the love of Christ that he said, "For Christ's love compels us."[2] How unfortunate that many of us are constrained by expectations of certain levels of performance rather than by God's love.

One of the greatest hindrances that keeps us from experiencing Christ's love is the tendency to serve ourselves. When life begins, we cry, "I need." Then quickly we change to, "I want." We are concerned only about ourselves. By our whimpers, cries, pouts, and demands, we say, "I am the most important person alive." Only Christ can make us a part of something much bigger than ourselves. It is a long, hard road from being self-pleasing to being Christ-pleasing.

Even our own desire for holiness may be selfish. It may be rooted in self-centeredness rather than, "May Jesus be glorified."

A self-centered person talks more about what God has done for him than about what Christ can do for others. He or she is concerned about the cares of life while a Christ-centered person rejoices in the riches of God. A self-centered individual talks about his desire for love, joy, and peace while someone who is Christ-centered talks about Jesus. A self-centered person talks about his own private convictions while the Christ-centered person talks about the love of God. A self-centered person speaks of his own personal sanctification, while a Christ-centered person speaks of the Gospel.

Even the songs we sing reflect this self-orientation: "Give *me* oil in *my* lamp, keep *me* burning." "*I've* got the joy, joy, joy." "*I'm* so glad *I'm* a part of the family of God." "Oh, that will be glory for *me*." Most of what we talk and sing about focuses on us and reveals the direction in which our interests lie. Notice the difference when we focus on him. Our singing becomes, "Isn't *He* wonderful, wonderful, wonderful." "Worship *His* Majesty." "Blessed be the *Lord God Almighty*." "How great *Thou* art."

Unless Christ rightfully becomes the center of our attention, we defraud him.

Maturity Through Suffering

Paul Rees suggests, "To *endure* hardship with a soothed and strengthened spirit is much: to *employ* hardship so that it actually becomes useful, both to ourselves and to others, is greatly more!"[3]

Why do Christians suffer? No doubt there are many reasons. The easiest to understand is *the law of sowing and reaping*. Or we might call it *the law of cause and effect*. It means that if we do wrong things we can expect adversity in return. If we do evil we can expect evil results. Sometimes, however, we tend to believe that this is the only reason for suffering, and that every wrong in life has someone or something to which we can ascribe immediate blame. That is a dangerous mistake to make.

Another reason for suffering is that *Satan is the ruler of the world and a destroyer*. Working diligently through demon agents, he sets about to destroy God's wonderful human creation. He works through specific one-on-one attacks in which demons array themselves against individuals, as well as through the world system where he has influenced countless numbers of people to adversely influence others.

A third reason for suffering is *the chastening of the Lord*. We might call it Christian boot camp. Its design is to get us ready for war; it removes whatever is unnecessary in the life of a soldier-in-training, and the "toughening up" process often involves pain.

W. W. Payson said, "Pain has other and higher functions than penalty," for "the outer man must be sacrificed in the interests of the man within, and the world of man without, and the unseen worlds beyond."[4]

This does not mean God is pleased when people suffer, let alone when his own people hurt. In fact, the evidence is that he abhors suffering and sorrow. But we live in a world of turmoil, a world that is engaged in a powerful spiritual struggle. Knowing that, God has warned us of potential pain. Nowhere does the Bible suggest that while we are here on earth we can come to a place of total ease, a place of complete tranquillity.

Christians are the Enemy's prime targets. When difficulties come, the Enemy sometimes attempts to convince us it is because of our "weak faith." Discouragement may follow and faith may be shaken.

Jesus informed Peter that Satan wanted to put him to the test. Years later, Peter wrote to fellow believers telling them that Satan goes about as a roaring lion seeking to destroy whomever he can.[5] We remember that phrase likening Satan to a roaring lion, but sometimes we forget what Peter went on to say: "And the God of all grace, who called you to his eternal glory in Christ, *after you have suffered a little while*, will himself restore you and make you strong, firm and steadfast" (italics added).[6] "Dear friends, do not be surprised at the *painful trial you are suffering*, as though something strange were happening to you. But rejoice that you participate in the sufferings of Christ, so that you may be overjoyed when his glory is revealed" (italics added).[7]

Paul the Apostle also acknowledged that, for the Christian, suffering was inevitable: "*We also rejoice in our sufferings*, because we know that suffering produces perseverance; perseverance, character; and character, hope. . . ."[8] Paul was thankful to God for allowing him to be a soldier in the conflict and for allowing him to suffer for Christ's sake. The great British preacher Charles Spurgeon said, "The Lord gets his best soldiers out of the highlands of affliction."

Pain can actually make us better people. Pain pushes our roots deep enough so that we need not be constantly watered by the assurances of people around us.

Paul also told the Corinthians that "*our light and momentary troubles are achieving for us* an eternal glory that far outweighs them all."[9] In the same letter he wrote, "Praise be to the God and Father of our Lord Jesus Christ, the Father of compassion and the God of all comfort, who comforts us *in all our troubles*, so that we can comfort those *in any trouble* with the comfort we ourselves have received from God. For just as *the sufferings of Christ flow over into our lives*, so also through Christ our comfort overflows."[10]

Jesus Christ himself told us that we would have trouble in this world, but he added, "Take heart! I have overcome the world."[11]

Learning to Overcome

How do we become overcomers with him?

It takes more than just shouting "glory" and telling the devil where to go. It involves commitment to Christ, a right attitude, and teaching, understanding, and discipline. And it never happens outside of the dimension of Christ's Spirit living within us. Of all of the things that are necessary for victory—the armor of God, praise, worship, prayer, obedience, the blood of the Lamb, the Word of God, the Name of Jesus—nothing will happen if the Spirit of Christ is not active in us.

We sometimes tire of the pressures we face while trying to live the Christian life. Jeremiah the Prophet was no different; he was worn down too. Finally, when he complained to God, God told him, "If you have raced with men on foot and they have worn you out, how can you compete with horses? If you stumble in safe country, how will you manage in the thickets by the Jordan?"[12]

The attitude of the Israelites while under Egyptian bondage is noteworthy for insight into overcoming: "But the more they were oppressed, the more they multiplied and spread."[13]

Another important aspect of overcoming lies in determining the source of our problem. As we have already noted, Satan causes problems, the flesh produces pain, and God chastens. Never attribute to one source or another what the Holy Spirit has not made perfectly clear. It is dangerous to assume that God has brought adversity when it was really the Enemy. To assume that Satan is to blame when our own sinfulness has gotten us into trouble is likewise unproductive.

Satan is to be resisted. The flesh is to be mastered by the spirit, and God's discipline is not to be taken lightly. Learning which is which is not easy, but it is so very necessary if we are to overcome.

Few of the battles faced by a true overcomer are simple. Most strike with the force of a raging hurricane. Try, for instance, to forgive when someone has terribly wronged you, perhaps through a divorce or a bad business deal. Or try to figure out what to do when you are a victim of gossip or when your best friend has forsaken you.

Paul Rees comments:

> We sometimes imagine that the good life, if it be con-
> sistent, will shut the mouth of every critic and close the
> eyes of every fault-finder. Unfortunately that is not so.
> There are plenty of people in this world so morally color-
> blind that they would mistake the white pinions of an
> angel for the black wings of a crow. So it is that the
> misunderstood Christ appeals to us, not as some strange
> Being far removed from the hurly-burly of our common
> life but as One who stands among us, with the scars of
> life's conflict upon Him and the sympathy of love and
> understanding within Him.[14]

Three Stages of Christian Development

Sooner or later, the heart that begins its advance toward God usually finds that the joy of initial salvation has somehow melted like an ice-cream cone on a hot summer day. When we first began, there was sheer delight, wonderful joy, and so much to learn. We were excited. The world lay before us and our stout hearts said, "We will conquer it for Jesus." Enthusiasm abounded. We had entered *the blessing and excitement stage*. Every day was bright and sunny and the manifestations of God's love were abundant. The mountain streams of his blessings satisfied to the depths of our souls. Refreshing breezes from his Word whispered, "I will never leave you nor forsake you." Then suddenly a desert appeared, a vast wilderness full of temptations, trials, suffering, and sorrow. We had entered *the desert stage*. Had God arbitrarily left us, or had we somehow neglected him so that he retreated? Where did he go? How did we get so far from him?

Desert experiences are hot, dry, and lonely. Body, soul, and spirit cry out for the streams that are now only a fading memory. There is not a soldier in God's army who has not cried out in pain, wondering how much more he could take. Finally, however, when the desert is crossed, we find that the other side contains the wonderful mountain heights we so desired. We are in *the communion stage*. Here, as we climb in sweet fellowship with God, we see the reason for his ways. The desert we now tower above is strewn with baggage and goods that would have made the present climb impossible. That wasteland is filled with the cares of this life, aspirations for greatness, selfishness, pride, and dozens of other worthless articles that weighed us down.

How we wish that once the last stage was entered, we could stay there for eternity. But as long as we are in the flesh, we find we are ever cycling through these three stages of development. How marvelous are the ways of God as he seeks to detach us from the world, the flesh, and the devil so that we might be attached to him.

A Place of Rest and Blessing

Are you growing in the grace of God? Have degrees of understanding, wisdom, and knowledge been added to your life in recent weeks and months? Are the fruits of the Spirit getting stronger while replacing the works of the flesh? Are you able to draw strength from the Lord so that your character is enriched unto greater hope, or do the trials of life make you negative, bitter, and critical?

If you are having trouble in any of these areas, immediately make a threefold commitment to prayer, Bible study, and fellowship with God's people. By doing so you will move, even if somewhat slowly, to a place of rest and blessing in him.

☖5☖
The Ministry of Jesus Christ

His Ministry Was to Serve

Most kings and noblemen are born in palaces and places of grandeur. Jesus, the King of kings, was born in a smelly stable where you couldn't walk a straight line without stepping into trouble.

Kings are born and raised in royal cities. Jesus was born in lowly Bethlehem and raised in Nazareth, a city which carried a stigma and prompted the question, "Can anything good come out of Nazareth?"

The births of kings are announced to entire nations. The birth of Jesus was announced to only a handful of people.

Kings learn to use servants for their own purpose. Jesus became a servant to save lost humanity.

The chief characteristic of a king is his power. The chief characteristic of Jesus is his love.

Kings do not associate with common people. Jesus grew up

among the poor and needy and associated with them freely.

Everything about Jesus lay in stark contrast to what was expected of royalty. No wonder he brought confusion and question to so many, including many of those who followed him. He did nothing in the manner of a king, and yet the awaited Messiah was the King of kings.

The King who came to conquer had stooped to become a servant in order to enter the door of the human heart. At the root of all of humanity's problems lay a soiled existence that no amount of dictatorial rule would ever cleanse. The worst of human bondage lay not in oppression by an earthly tyrant but from the Enemy of man's soul and from the defilement of the human heart.

The Creator knew that man's rebellion, the thing that prevented his healing, would be broken only by a tremendous act of humility on God's part. And so the King, in love, became a servant.

Timed According to God's Plan

Although Christ's actual ministry did not begin until he was about thirty years of age, years before, at the age of twelve, he had proven his ability to handle the Scriptures. Why he waited so long before he began to preach is not revealed. Whatever the reason, God had a time schedule for his plan and it included a man named John the Baptist.

About six months prior to the birth of Jesus, John was born of godly parents, Zechariah and Elizabeth, who were fellow countrymen of Joseph and Mary.

During Mary's visit to Elizabeth's home, God filled Elizabeth with his Holy Spirit. She was pregnant with John, and upon Mary's entrance she loudly exclaimed, "Blessed are you among women, and blessed is the child you will bear! But why am I so favored, that the mother of my Lord should come to me? As soon as the sound of your greeting reached my ears, the baby in my womb leaped for joy. Blessed is she who has believed that what the Lord has said to her will be accomplished!"[1]

Mary responded, "My soul glorifies the Lord and my spirit rejoices in God my Savior, for he has been mindful of the humble state of his servant. From now on all generations will call me blessed, for the Mighty One has done great things for me—holy is his name."[2]

A few months after Mary's visit, John was born. He grew up to be a rugged individual, dressed in clothes made from camel's hair and eating locusts and wild honey. With a prophet's call, he preached in the Desert of Judea, proclaiming "a baptism of repentance for the forgiveness of sins."[3]

John's primary task was to go before Jesus and bear witness that He was the Light God was sending into the world. Mark records, "It is written in Isaiah the prophet: 'I will send my messenger ahead of you, who will prepare your way'—'a voice of one calling in the desert, "Prepare the way for the Lord, make straight paths for him." ' "[4]

From far and near, people came to hear John's message. Many were eventually baptized in the Jordan River as a sign of their repentance of sins. Although John gained fame rapidly, he carefully directed attention to the One he had been called to glorify: " 'I baptize with water,' John replied, 'but among you stands one you do not know. He is the one who comes after me, the thongs of whose sandals I am not worthy to untie.' "[5]

"The next day John saw Jesus coming toward him and said, 'Look, the Lamb of God, who takes away the sin of the world! This is the one I meant when I said, "A man who comes after me has surpassed me because he was before me." I myself did not know him, but the reason I came baptizing with water was that he might be revealed to Israel.' "[6]

With the revelation of Jesus, John's ministry was completed. His testimony had sufficiently declared the Son of God when he said, "I saw the Spirit come down from heaven as a dove and remain on him. I would not have known him, except that the one who sent me to baptize with water told me, 'The man on whom you see the Spirit come down and remain is he who will baptize with the Holy Spirit.' I have seen and I testify that this is the Son of God."[7]

After Jesus had been baptized in water by John and also with the Holy Spirit by the Father, the Spirit of God led him into the desert. There, for forty days, he fasted while being tempted of the devil. The devil then tempted him to turn a stone into a piece of bread. Appealing to his natural senses, the Enemy tried to get Jesus to use his authority and power for self-serving purposes. But Jesus answered, "It is written: 'Man does not live on bread alone.' "[8] We could never identify with Christ if he had used his deity to overcome.

The devil then took him to a high place, showed him all the kingdoms of the world, and said, "I will give you all their authority and splendor, for it has been given to me, and I can give it to anyone I want to. So if you worship me, it will all be yours."[9] Perhaps Satan showed Jesus the major ruling demons who were controlling geographical areas of the world. Jesus would be over all other rebellious demons, subject only to Satan himself, if he would worship him. Again Jesus refused the temptation: "It is written: 'Worship the Lord your God and serve him only.' "[10]

Finally, the devil led Jesus to the highest point on the temple in Jerusalem, where he said, "If you are the Son of God, throw yourself down from here. For it is written: 'He will command his angels concerning you to guard you carefully; they will lift you up in their hands, so that you will not strike your foot against a stone.' " Jesus answered, "It says: 'Do not put the Lord your God to the test.' "[11]

Satan is a master at presenting half-truths. He was quick to point out what guardian angels would do without mentioning the preceding part of the Scripture, which says, "If you make the Most High your dwelling—even the Lord, who is my refuge—then no harm will befall you, no disaster will come near your tent. For he will command his angels. . . ."[12]

We must be careful not to tempt divine government. We cannot sacrifice the commands of God on the altar of a steady faith in order to receive a greater faith. Neither are we to request a change in the principles and order of the universe in order to satisfy selfish curiosity. It is all too easy to desire a miracle only to develop an interest in our own ministry— really our own selves.

Do not conclude that because Jesus was God, his temptation was any less significant than ours. In reality it was much greater. *The greater the purity in a life, the more there will be a hatred of sin and a resistance to temptation. This greater resistance makes the intensity much stronger.*

We sometimes conclude we are doing poorly spiritually because we are struggling with temptation. The very strain is an indication we have not given in and are moving ahead spiritually.

With this last temptation, Satan was done with Jesus for a time. But he was by no means through with him completely. He would be back. Meanwhile, Jesus returned to civilization preaching, teaching, and doing miracles in the power of the Holy Spirit. He healed the sick, raised the dead, and cast out demons. Nothing like this had ever been seen before. The kingdom of heaven had come to earth.

The Message of the Kingdom

For the next three years, Jesus preached the kingdom of heaven among men. He preached righteousness, holiness, eternal life, and judgment, as he carefully introduced his kingdom to earth. He made it quite clear that although he was the Creator, he had not been in control of the planet since Adam had given it to Satan a long time ago: "Now is the time for judgment on this world; now the prince of this world will be driven out."[13] He had come to begin the reclamation of the planet, beginning with its inhabitants. He came to save what was lost, to bring light and life into our realm of death and darkness. John says that God "did not send his Son into the world to condemn the world, but to save the world through him."[14]

No one could see, at that time, the incredible amount of darkness in the world. So defiled is our planet that Jesus had to declare war on it. His words roused opposition: "Do you think I came to bring peace on earth? No, I tell you, but division."[15]

Certainly he stirred up the people. He meant to do so. He could never preach the status quo while people lived and participated in a world of wrong. Injustice, oppression, hypocrisy, and sham of every kind were his targets. This new kingdom had marked the old one for replacement.

What makes some Christians quite different from others is the same unabashed, unabated, no-kid-gloves challenge of evil that was in Christ. If we are to succeed in our endeavors for him, there needs to be in us a daring honesty to confront and make uncomfortable every form of egotistical self-satisfaction.

Personally Concerned About People

Jesus was personally concerned about individuals, especially the common man. He walked among the masses and ate with publicans and sinners. He was no recluse.

His primary interest was that men be saved, but he was also concerned about their personal needs in the here and now. He healed a royal official's son. He healed a man by the pool of Bethesda. At one time he healed ten lepers. He cast a demon out of a young boy. He raised a man named Lazarus who had been dead for four days. Matthew says that "Jesus went throughout Galilee, teaching in their synagogues, preaching the good news of the kingdom, and healing every disease and sickness among the people."[16]

6
Christian Ministry

The Heart of Christian Ministry: Love

Love is the true mark of discipleship. Jesus said, "A new command I give you: Love one another. As I have loved you, so you must love one another. By this all men will know that you are my disciples, if you love one another."[1]

It is very tragic that many people insist on other identifying marks as a means of identifying with Christ: the way they dress, the church they attend, the pastor they follow, their denomination, their faithfulness, and more. Holiness, righteousness, and the commands of Christ are incredibly important, but there is only one credential for introducing one of Jesus' disciples: love.

The words *I love you* are very important. They are humbling words that make us vulnerable. They tear down our defenses and lay us bare before the person to whom we speak. They are the words of a kneeling heart. They are the mark of a servant. For the words to have real meaning they must be preceded by and backed up with actions that attest to what has been said. Love is first and foremost an action rather than a feeling. John said it this way: "Dear children, let us not love with words or tongue but with actions and in truth."[2]

With the many laws, rules, and commandments of the Word of God, we must be careful not to miss its overall intent, which Jesus says amounts to two commandments: "Love the Lord your God with all your heart and with all your soul and with all your mind and with all your strength" and "Love your neighbor as yourself."[3] It is amazing that as complicated as God's Word sometimes appears, it all boils down to loving God and others.

Since love is action more than feeling, what things bear witness to its presence? Paul wrote to the Corinthians to describe its characteristics: "Love is patient, love is kind. It does not envy, it does not boast, it is not proud. It is not rude, it is not self-seeking, it is not easily angered, it keeps no record of wrongs. Love does not delight in evil but rejoices with the truth. It always protects, always trusts, always hopes, always perseveres."[4]

We will never effectively join our hands in Christian work until we join our hearts in Christian love.

The Method of Christian Ministry: Servanthood

Many of the great people of the world have been noted for such traits as eloquence of speech, creativity, musical ability, economic insights, and political genius. Such abilities often have brought them fame and fortune. But it is not so in the kingdom of heaven. Here greatness has a completely different set of qualifications. "Whoever wants to become great among you must be your servant, and whoever wants to be first must be slave of all."[5]

It may seem strange, but the methods of the world are contrary to the methods and means of the kingdom Jesus came to reveal. And unless we allow him to introduce us to this new style of living, we will not only doubt its legitimacy but we will shrink from its operations as well.

Servanthood is completely foreign to our view of a successful life-style. It appears to be on the bottom rung of the ladder, if it is even on the ladder at all. Indeed, if you are unsuccessful in life, the only option remaining for you is service. It seems the only good thing about servanthood is that it has little competition. You won't find stacks of applications for the job. Nor will you find people walking on each other to move higher in the ranks. But such a calling cannot be bad when you consider two things: first, Jesus asks us to do it, and second, he was not above doing it himself.

Ministry Established by the Holy Spirit

When a person receives Christ as Lord and Savior, he becomes a part of the universal body of Christ. Within that body he has a specific place where God wants him to be, as well as a specific definable responsibility God has chosen to give to him. Finding this place and its responsibilities is one of our greatest challenges. It is not as difficult, however, as we are sometimes led to believe. One of the chief problems concerns our preconceived ideas about what ministry should be.

Many people have the mistaken idea that ministry needs to be public in order to please God, and we assume that working for him is more important than developing intimacy with him. In fact, the opposite is true: one of the greatest dangers to true devotion to Jesus is working for him. In other words, the great danger to "intimacy" is "ministry."

Although every believer is to have a ministry, that ministry is to be a consequence and outflow of a personal relationship with Jesus. Anything else springs from self-effort. There is nothing quite so meaningless and unfulfilling as constant motion that accomplishes nothing because we are moving outside of an intimate relationship with God. The great decisions in life do not involve determining what we can do for God but rather finding how he will work in us. God wants to give to us before we give to others.

Beginning According to God's Timing

Author G. Campbell Morgan said:

> The same Lord is still choosing, calling, and appointing. I cannot choose to be a missionary or a Christian minister. I must be chosen. The restfulness of this consideration lies in the fact that His choices and His calls are vindications. If He called me, I know it; and if He has called me, He has chosen me. Every day that I live I wonder more why He called me; but I know He did, and therein is my rest, my peace. My brothers and sisters within the Christian church, you cannot elect to serve. But if He has elected and called you, a solemn responsibility rests upon you. I urge you: Be of good cheer, for if He calls, it is because He has chosen, and your responsibility is only that of yielding.

God has a time for everything, especially for ministry in the life of a believer. His desire is that men be trained adequately before they assume certain responsibilities. In this way they avoid the danger of becoming conceited and of falling under the same condemnation as the devil (1 Timothy 3:6).

When the Lord places each person in the body, they are to assume certain light responsibilities almost immediately. As time goes on and they mature in the things of the Lord, these responsibilities increase. It is very important that we do not assume obligations which do not belong to us. This is frequently done when there appears to be no one else to do the job. Neither guilt nor pride should ever be the motivating force behind the decision leading to a place of ministry. If no one is there to do the job and God does not tell you to do it, leave it alone. God assumes far more responsibility for running the Church than most of us believe. Let him take the responsibility of filling the void. On the other hand, it is foolish to reject responsibilities that God has called us to accept. This is often done because of a feeling of inadequacy. God gives strength and ability for whatever he asks.

To make a person a Christian leader overnight when he simply does not have the spiritual maturity necessary to function properly is sheer foolishness. Often it is selfish exploitation. Not only is his or her spiritual life in danger but also the lives of those who look to that person for leadership. No amount of success in the natural realm will guarantee success in Christian leadership. God's word warns us against this in 1 Timothy chapter 3. It is easy to come quickly to a place of being able to articulate the Gospel faster than we are able to mature into it.

Another great danger for those desiring to do something for the Lord is getting ahead of his timetable. Impatience should be a key warning sign that something is amiss. It isn't that God hasn't called—it's that we haven't allowed him to train us sufficiently before we move out. If God was not in a hurry to get the ministry of Jesus into full swing, it is safe to assume there may be times we find that we are asked to wait.

Preparing for Ministry

Preparation for ministry is secondary to both our consecration to Jesus and our families. Many ministries have failed because Jesus was not kept at the center. Others have come to ruin because the leader's family was neglected. It is all too easy to sacrifice personal responsibility toward loved ones on an altar of ministry.

Service for Christ must never be in competition with devotion to him. With that in mind, here are six important considerations for being properly prepared:

1. *We must learn to seek the Lord.* It is easy to seek faith, blessing, position, honor, notoriety, security, wealth, and a variety of other things before we seek the Lord. Even for our defense in warfare we must be careful not to seek first the armor of God, but rather the God of our armor.

God is to be found in his Word, in prayer, and among his people. Interestingly enough, he can also be found among the hungry, the thirsty, strangers, the needy, the sick, and those in prison.

To find him, however, we need to press past religion, past hurts and pain, and past people. The woman with the issue of blood was healed when she pressed past the crowds that hindered her and finally touched Jesus.

2. *We must learn to handle the Word of God correctly.* Paul told Timothy, "Do your best to present yourself to God as one approved, a workman who does not need to be ashamed and who correctly handles the word of truth."[6] It takes much time to put the history, culture, poetry, and prophecy of the Bible together in such a way that we get God's clear meaning and

intent. Many good men have developed devastating theologies because they took the Word out of context.

3. *We must learn to pray.* Praying does not come easy. Nor is it always obvious what prayer is all about and what it accomplishes. Prayer is much more than just asking God for things. S. D. Gordon had learned well the meaning of prayer when he explained, "to adequately define prayer, one must use the language of war." The noted author went on to say, "Peace language is not equal to the situation. The earth is in a state of war and is being hotly besieged. Thus, one must use war talk to grasp the fact with which prayer is concerned. Prayer from God's side is communication between Himself and His allies in the enemy country."

Satan wants to destroy our relationship with God. He springs immediately to cut our lines of communication with the Lord. The Enemy of our soul is out to destroy us completely by keeping us from God. There is a war going on, and because we do not understand the war, we do not understand the necessity for prayer.

4. *We must learn to deal with sin.* Satan seizes every opportunity to quicken an inappropriate thought, polishing it to a luster that becomes desire, and fanning that desire into an obsession which clouds the mind and dims the spirit. Put more simply, if a man wishes not to be kicked he must not sit behind his cow. If temptation is not to be lodged in the heart, it must not be looked upon with a wandering eye.

Another great enemy is pride. We have made the commitment to live holy lives, and all of a sudden we are entangled once again in sin. We are embarrassed. Even worse, we are humiliated. We may not have thought it could happen to us. We were above failure, or at least we wanted to be. But it did happen, even when we were determined it would not. The maturing Christian finds that he makes many mistakes, but if he communicates these failures to the Lord, he will find that God is gracious to forgive.

5. *We must learn to deal with rebellion.* Our old nature has been so affected by rebellion that we tend to revert to old ways under the influence of the Enemy. The old nature will raise its ugly head whenever possible. Believers must constantly deal with the temptation to rebel.

6. *We must learn to fellowship with God's people.* We make some dangerous assumptions in Christianity. We suppose that certain Christians have "arrived" in their quest for God. We build them up in our minds, believing they undoubtedly have reached a pinnacle of perfection. When they slip, we are devastated.

We presume that everyone loves everyone else and that it is impossible to get hurt within the body of Christ. Then when we find viciousness and vindictiveness in the Church, we are shocked. The hurt and pain can cause severe emotional wounds.

King David was faithful to sing, "How good and pleasant it is when brothers live together in unity!"[7] God doesn't just "hope" we will get along with other believers—he demands it. The Apostle Paul, writing to the Ephesians, declared, "I warn you, as I did before, that those who live like this will not inherit the kingdom of God."[8] Live like what? Paul said that a person who *practiced* hatred, discord, jealousy, fits of rage, dissensions, factions, and envy was not saved.

Why Some Ministry Fails

The most common reason ministry fails has to do with a lack of love. I'm not speaking about a lack of feeling but the failure to do what must be done to meet the needs of people.

Feelings go up and down like the tides of the ocean, and they are generally deceiving.

Most people need a certain amount of excitability in order to function in ministry. However, the most effective people in ministry have learned to move forward *as an act of their will.* They don't need a sensation in order to be obedient to righteousness; nor are they the ones who move only as the spirit moves them or only as they hear from God in some vision or dream. They walk among the needy and the wounded and with God's help assess the needs in order to properly meet them.

Another common reason for failure in personal ministry has to do with self-effort. Jesus said, "Apart from me you can do nothing."[9] We need to draw directly from him constantly. The indwelling of the Holy Spirit is not a one-time experience. It is an empowering to accomplish what is impossible within human ability alone.

There are other reasons ministry fails:

1. *We are too busy with the cares of this life.* Caring for others can become a side issue if we become overly involved in the things of this world. Providing for the basic necessities of life is essential. The problem arises when worry and faithlessness to God result from an overconcern for our own personal well-being.

2. *We have too many toys.* If children were the only ones who had toys, our world would be a very dull place. Adults need them too. But many grown-ups acquire so many that they waste most of their lives playing with them.

3. *We have misplaced priorities.* Failure to give time to the things that are most important results in all kinds of failures. Good is often the enemy of best.

4. *We delight in the gifts and countenances of men.* Ministry is the outgrowth of servanthood. It is bestowed upon those who

are in a position to give rather than to receive—those who have already received from the Lord. Its entire nature is to be void of self-seeking. Ministry was never meant to be a way of meeting our own needs. It is not to be a means whereby we receive what we are short of, either emotionally or materially. The Prophet Isaiah warned, "Your rulers are rebels, companions of thieves; they all love bribes and chase after gifts. They do not defend the cause of the fatherless; the widow's case does not come before them."[10]

5. *We fail to prepare properly before we minister.* To offer advice about that which we have little knowledge is both foolish and dangerous. To take full responsibility for something we are unfamiliar with is not wise. Study and experience help to make us channels of God's blessing for supplying the needs of others. There is nothing wrong with indicating we do not know some things, but it is important that we endeavor to learn the truth wholeheartedly.

6. *We are not diligent.* Lack of dependability prevents the trust that is necessary for establishing good relationships. A person who keeps his word is one to whom others are much more willing to listen. Late appointments, inaccurate statements, an air of aloofness, forgetfulness, and misuse of time all have adverse effects upon our ability to touch the lives of others.

7. *We are ignorant of what God is doing universally.* Tunnel vision is a major deterrent to the cause of Christ. It allows narrow-mindedness to raise its ugly head and boast, "If God is not working in us, he can't be working." Foolish is the person who believes he stands at the head of the column in God's army.

8. *We allow certain destructive attitudes and mind-sets to prevail.* When we display attitudes of superiority, harshness, perfectionism, etc., we make it difficult for others to receive our

communication. True ministry is the product of one-directional love. It is a love that flows out to others without the slightest need for anything in return. Its nature is to give without the necessity to receive. When giving has attached to it any other motive than the good of the individual to whom it is being directed, it is not of God.

People who give only because it is their responsibility have not found the joy of true ministry. But the man or woman who is learning to give because someone has a need is learning to represent the heart of God.

9. *We do not understand how God leads his people.* In the Old Testament, the Spirit of the Lord came upon men and women, anointing them to speak the heart and mind of God. These people were called prophets. In the New Testament, God's Spirit has been given to every person who knows Jesus. It is no longer one person but the collective body of Christ through which God reveals himself. An individual, however, is still needed for leadership, and frequently God will speak through this one person. But the message will always be affirmed by others in the body, those who have learned to listen to the Lord. Jack Hayford says that God gives direction but man gives confirmation.

A wise body of believers will at times allow God to speak to them through other believers outside their own group, believers who have proven abilities to listen to God.

Only a foolish person rejects advice. Yet some individuals claim that God is their only counsel and they need no other. God has placed us in his body, where we are expected to protect one another. Godly counsel is not only good, it is also necessary because it is biblical. This kind of safeguard keeps us from being deceived.

All too often, a person wrongly believes he has heard from the Lord and then proceeds to force his will upon the rest of the body of believers. In the process, the spirits of many believers are quenched. Quenching the Spirit has more to do with one's approach to the collective body of Christ than to some supposed disobedience to the leading and guidance of the Holy Spirit.

10. *We allow legalism or liberalism to replace the grace which is in Jesus Christ.* Whenever holiness is legislated from without or neglected from within, whenever it fails to take on the form of the Holy Spirit working in our lives, whenever it fails to be built on both love for God and man, it serves as nothing more than self-righteousness.

The Character of the Person Who Ministers

Christians who expound truth found in the Word of God are themselves to be an expression of that truth. Granted, none of us is perfect in the sense of being flawless. But we are to come to a place in Christ where we are above reproach, where we are temperate, self-controlled, and respectable. Faithfulness, righteousness, and accountability must be carefully developed.

Knowledge of Bible truth alone does not qualify one for leadership. A person short on character development must receive careful supervision as he develops his ministry. This must continue until he has proven himself to be reliable. And although we may grow to a place of reliability, we never outgrow our need for accountability.

Can a person who has failed morally be restored to leadership? Without question, the answer is yes. Both David and Moses were men of great failure (murder), yet both went on to lead God's people. In the New Testament, Peter denied Christ, yet was renewed.

Many times the moral failure of a leader is a problem of character. In such cases, restoration begins with confession and repentance. This is the beginning, not the end, of recovery. Character must be rebuilt, and in humility the fallen leader begins the road to a reestablishment of trust. But he will never be seen as reliable if he is not willing to own up to his sin.

Fulfilling God's Purpose

Do you see ministry as leadership or as servanthood? Your answer may determine whether or not you will truly be used by God in his service. Although many servants eventually become leaders, becoming a leader must never be our primary goal. Fulfillment of God's purpose in our lives is not found in telling people what to do or in becoming an "important" figure. *A person finds true ministry and real fulfillment only by adding to someone else's life.*

7
Jesus in Gethsemane

On the first day of the Feast of Unleavened Bread, Jesus ate the Passover supper with his disciples. It was during this time of fellowship that Judas Iscariot was exposed. He would be the one to betray Jesus that very night.

After they had finished supper, Jesus and the disciples went out of the city toward the Mount of Olives to a small garden area called Gethsemane. Here, in the stillness of the night, Jesus suffered much in his preparation to take upon himself the sin of the world. In another garden, long before, another man wrestled with sin, only to fail his entire race. But in this second garden, this "second Adam" would move to set humanity free from the bondage incurred in that first garden.

A Very Real Battle

For whatever else Gethsemane may have been, it certainly was a battlefield. "Overwhelmed with sorrow to the point of death,"[1] Jesus asked his followers for help. None of them, however, recognized the immensity of the events that were now unfolding. Heavy with sleep, they rested while Jesus wrestled. We do not know precisely what went on as Jesus struggled, but we know it was an intense moment. For his sweat to come forth as great drops of blood indicates tremendous personal agony. No doubt he was once again face-to-face with Satan, as he had been in the wilderness only a few years before.

The time for which Jesus had come to earth was at hand. The cross he would face shortly had been a part of God's plan for man's redemption for thousands of years. Now it was about to become a reality. From the beginning, God knew that only such an event would release mankind from his horrible bondage to sin and Satan. But something in Jesus shrank at the commission. "My Father," he cried, "if it is possible, may this cup be taken from me. Yet not as I will, but as you will."[2]

Was the human factor now pressing in upon him? Did he pull back from death because that is the natural tendency of all men? Did failure enter his mind? Did he recognize that soon he would be in the grasp of hell itself and that he would have to wage a tremendous warfare there?

Perhaps the real reason Jesus hesitated had to do with his relationship with the Father. If he were to take upon himself the sin of the world, the Father would be forced to turn his back on him. The "cup" he wanted removed was a symbol of the sin and suffering of a lost world. To drink it would force the Father to look away. His heaviness, no doubt, came from the thought of becoming sin and being removed, even if temporarily, from the presence of the Father.

Sinlessness was facing sin. The horribleness of sin that Christ was about to take upon himself cut deeply into his sensitive spirit. The Lamb of God was about to be slain in order to take away the sin of the world.

With keen insight, Herschel Hobbs comments:

> This suggests the abyss into which, in that moment, Jesus was plunged. To be separated from and forsaken by God is hell. That is why Jesus cried, "My God, my God, why hast thou forsaken me?" The final, irrevocable fruit of sin is to be God-forsaken. Thus our Lord in that moment endured all the agonies of hell. Though it was but for a moment as men reckon time, it was the infinite entrance of an infinite God into the infinite agonies of hell which is the just due of every sinner.[3]

Walking over to his disciples and finding them asleep, Jesus said to Peter, "Could you men not keep watch with me for one hour? Watch and pray so that you will not fall into temptation. The spirit is willing, but the body is weak."[4]

Going away a second time, he prayed, "My Father, if it is not possible for this cup to be taken away unless I drink it, may your will be done."[5] When he returned, again he found them sleeping. Leaving them, he went away a third time to pray.

Jesus Is Arrested

A short time later, a large crowd sent from the chief priests and other leaders of the Jewish people proceeded to arrest Jesus. Flickering lights and dancing shadows told of the advancing mob. Accompanying them was one of his disciples, Judas Iscariot, whose intent was to betray Christ into the hands of those who sought to have him put to death. In a fury of anger and hatred, armed men with swords and clubs moved in to arrest Jesus. But Peter "reached for his sword, drew it out and struck the servant of the high priest, cutting off his ear."[6] "Jesus commanded Peter, 'Put your sword away! Shall I not drink the cup the Father has given me?' "[7]

Notice the words *shall I not drink the cup.* Shortly before, Jesus had asked the Father to remove his cup of suffering if it were possible. Recognizing, however, that there was no other way to complete his mission, and knowing that he must fulfill his Father's will, he proceeded with steadfast resolve.

Prayer had brought him this release. When he speaks to Peter, he is determined to be obedient. He had come to earth in total dedication to the will of the Father, and his struggle would guarantee that he would remain that way.

8
Gethsemane Experiences

The Purpose

In Gethsemane, the will of the Father was the crucial issue.
It is still the issue that drives men and women into Gethsemane experiences today. Confused by the questions of life,
we too are driven into this garden plot. And only a Gethsemane experience will cause a person to say, "I seek not to
please myself but him who sent me."

It was the will of man that got him into trouble in the first
place, and it is the will of man that can get him out of trouble
in the end. I do not mean that we can will our own salvation
or that salvation can be accomplished by works. But a man
must be willing to let God save him if he is to be saved.

God is not interested in violating the human will. He refuses to force man to obey him. The closest he will come is to
allow us to be pressed to the point where we are compelled to
look closely at the consequences of the choices we make. It

must never be assumed that God is trying to change us in such a way that when our will lines up with his we will wind up completely miserable. Quite the opposite is true. And although the Enemy teaches that if it is unpleasant it must be the will of God, the psalmist affirmed, "I delight to do thy will, O my God: yea, thy law is within my heart."[1]

Everything that God allows to happen to us is for our good. *The trials we face, the sufferings we encounter, and the attacks of Satan all are in our best interests when they are allowed by God.*

Nothing the Lord does in regard to a child of God is ever done to hurt him, and nothing can happen to that child without God's permission. On the other hand, it is important that we do not allow the Enemy to go any further than the permission he has obtained from God.

In Gethsemane, a person will see better who he is. He will understand the fallacy of believing that somewhere in him there is innate goodness. Perhaps a Gethsemane experience caused Abraham to say, "I am nothing but dust and ashes."[2]

Gethsemane's Treasured Choices

The trauma of Gethsemane experiences can develop a depth that can be gained nowhere else. In the darkness of spiritual midnight, a few will wrestle with God in deep contrition until they come forth with a profoundness to their character unattainable through any other encounter. Here the most difficult of questions must be worked through. Here wants and desires must be analyzed in light of the countenance of God. Here the forces of hell try unrelentlessly to get us to abandon our allegiance to Christ. Here, however, most will walk away more thankful for the revelation of him than for any answer given. Some, though rejoicing, will walk away limping like Jacob, for a man will never again be the same after wrestling with God. And some will walk away acknowledging that "we win only when the will of God is done."

Gethsemane pleads with us to hoist the sails of our tiny ships and voyage from our sheltered and safe harbors out into the ocean of God. And although God bids, "Come, walk on the water," we tremble with the fear of losing the security of the ships we have built.

Unfortunately, others rebel in Gethsemane. Not understanding what God is allowing, they turn from him, instead of to him.

The world is full of injustices that strike at us. Sicknesses, plagues, financial setbacks, and various other sufferings and sorrows sometimes hit the best of God's servants. Missionary David Brainerd, renowned for his prayer life, was stricken with tuberculosis and died at just twenty-nine years of age. Yes, Satan wins many battles in this life, but we will win the war.

In Gethsemane, God will force the issue of sin. Sin is of grave concern to God because it destroys what man needs and what God wants—fellowship. God will not leave the question alone. He will continue his discourse until either we repent in humility or walk away in rebellion.

In Gethsemane, God asks for total allegiance: "You cannot serve two masters." The cares of this life, riches, honor, friends, whatever catches our attention, must be submitted because God asks that everything we put our hand to become second to him. God does not ask things of us in order to make us miserable. On the contrary, everything God does is designed for our deliverance from the things in life that cause pain.

In Gethsemane, we are asked to become soldiers in God's army. Here we learn the fight song of the cross. The armor of

the Lord is laid before us, and we must now choose to put
it on.

In Gethsemane, we discover a unique communications system called prayer and learn to use it, not for self-serving purposes but to communicate with the Captain of our salvation,
who sits at the right hand of the Father. Men and women who
have often been to Gethsemane are called prayer warriors.
Though their vision of the King is far from complete, glimpses
of him have caused them to seek him above all else.

Saints From Gethsemane

When you meet a person coming from Gethsemane, you
can be sure he is one in whom self-sufficiency is being destroyed. He realizes that the rush of activity regarded as a
necessity for success in this life is not a requirement for pleasing God. Through activity, we demand that we be useful to
God. The end of the matter is that we hold before him the
meager trophies of our self-effort in hopes that he will be
pleased. *God is not pleased by what we can do for him but by what
he can do for us.*

The most significant aspect of our salvation experience is
that we are to have a personal relationship with Jesus in which
he constantly gives to us the wonders of his personality.

This person from Gethsemane will be well acquainted with
quietness. He has found that God's silence is an effective tool
in developing discipline. It is often through silence that God
brings an individual into an understanding of himself. Only
when the soul is silenced (not passive) will the spirit truly
begin to hear.

The greatest gain from the seclusion of the garden lies in
the fact that there is now an unwavering conviction that God
is real. Abraham's journeys through barrenness and Moses'

years of waiting are no longer a mystery; they have become landmarks to guide us in our pilgrimage.

The person from Gethsemane is concerned about one thing above all else: fellowship with God. This is an individual who originally went to prayer seeking an answer. He now goes to prayer first to seek God. Where he once insisted upon a reply, he now wants to behold the Lord. He no longer demands happiness and joy from a sin-sick world but instead discovers them in the presence of the Lord. The cares of this life, the deceitfulness of riches, the pride of life, and scores of other intrusions are now seen as invasions capable of keeping him from the goal upon which he has set his heart. For defense, he has chosen to make the Spirit of God his steady companion.

In a world desiring information more than intimacy, it is far easier to listen to a testimony or a soothing sermon than to listen to God himself. It was said of the children of Israel at the foot of Mount Sinai, "they stayed at a distance and said to Moses, 'Speak to us yourself and we will listen. But do not have God speak to us or we will die.' "[3]

Gethsemane makes a person come face-to-face with the commandment "Trust in the Lord." Many people claim to have no serious doubt about what God can and will do as a Leader in their lives; they doubt only their own faith. That is fraudulent. We do not doubt ourselves. It is God we do not trust. In this Garden we draw from him the faith that says, "He is able."

God wants us to be like Christ—not that we are to lose our own identity, but that the richness of what he possesses might become ours as well. Continuing in the presence of the Lord produces a reflection of his image. The face of Moses, as he descended from the mount, contained so much of the Lord that it shone as a radiant glow.

Gethsemane is where a person is conformed to the likeness

of God's Son. Those who have been there find they often leave with marks that are witness of the hammer and anvil which gives shape to a new image. Paul said he bore on his body the "marks of Jesus."[4]

When the Road to Emmaus Winds Through Gethsemane

After the Crucifixion two of the disciples walked the road to Emmaus deeply troubled in spirit. The earlier events surrounding the cross had left them much discouraged. But when the Lord approached, even though they didn't recognize him, their hearts suddenly burned within as he spoke.

The desire for God that burns in our hearts is brought about by the presence of the Lord himself. Sometimes we think this deep yearning comes from our own personal motivation. This is hardly so.

Man never seeks God without first being drawn by his Spirit. What mankind wants has nothing to do with a desire for God. All hungering and thirsting is precipitated by a touch from the Holy Spirit. Failure to understand this truth may result in frustration and cause a person to miss the closeness of the Lord. We must realize that in sincerely wanting God, we already have him. We can't have *true* hunger without having him. We can't have a *real* desire for righteousness without having him.

To truly find Jesus in wonderful closeness takes time, and the paths to the mountaintop of his glory all wind through Gethsemane.

Will You Go to Gethsemane?

Are you ready to follow wherever Christ leads? There are certainly some wonderful places you will travel with him. And there are many glorious blessings he will bestow upon you. But because there is a war going on, he sometimes will ask things of you that seem difficult.

Can you handle disappointment? Can you face discouragement? Can you lay aside your temptation to reenter into rebellion when nothing seems to go right and you feel lonely and forsaken? Will you curse him because you are in great need and he doesn't seem to care? Or will you humbly continue to seek him in spite of the circumstances? Will you go to Gethsemane regardless?

9
Christ at Calvary

Part 1

Who can grasp the idea of God suffering? To us the words *God* and *suffer* do not and cannot coexist. They seem completely unrelated.

When we look at the figure on the cross, the one suffering in agony, the one who thirsts, the one whose blood runs from his veins, and utter, "My God," we appear to be in danger of monstrous blasphemy.

We look at him hanging there in disgrace and we are tempted to question and then to doubt. Instinctively, we want to try to take him down from the cross, to rescue him, to keep him from suffering and end this massive contradiction. Like Peter, we want to protect him from harm.

One thing is certain: nothing of the cross seems to make any sense. Where is God's majesty in this moment of shame? Where is God's omnipotence when a handful of soldiers jeer at him? Why is there no deliverance? Where is his terrifying magnificence? What is this disgrace? How completely unimaginable! What is the purpose of it all?

Covenant Relationship

People separated by race, color, creed, or other barriers often find themselves unable to get along with one another. Their mere association frequently creates trouble, even war. Therefore, mankind the world over has recognized the need for establishing peace treaties.

Many such treaties have been signed in blood. In fact, it appears that in the histories of most of the cultures of our world, somewhere there has been an understanding of the importance of making agreements through blood covenants.

The early American Indians made blood covenants (a covenant where blood functions as a seal in ratifying an agreement) with the first settlers. These kinds of covenants are considered very serious commitments because the parties recognize that if such a covenant is broken, it is in some cases to be satisfied by the shedding of the blood of the guilty party.

As adventurer and writer Henry Morton Stanley explored the wilds of Africa, he was often confronted with tribes of people willing to make peace with him through a "blood covenant." So well understood was the idea in the late 1800s as Stanley made his journeys that he reported his flesh was "cut" some fifty times in ceremonies with different tribal leaders in order to make agreements.

In one notable case, a covenant was made with one of Stanley's men, Frank Pocock, and a young tribal chief from Ntamo named Ngalyema (also called Itsi). Mr. Pocock's blood was to be substituted for Mr. Stanley's. After gifts were exchanged, the covenant ceremony began. In his book *Through the Dark Continent*, Stanley writes:

> The treaty with Itsi was exceedingly ceremonious, and involved the exchange of charms. Itsi transferred to me for my protection through life, a small gourdful of a curious powder, which had rather a saline taste; and I delivered over to him, as the white man's charm against all evil, a half-ounce vial of magnesia; further, a small scratch in Frank's arm, and another in Itsi's arm, supplied blood sufficient to unite us in one, and [by an] indivisible bond of fraternity.

This "proxy" or "substitutionary" blood was considered legal and binding upon Stanley himself, even though someone else stood in for him.

Some years later, Stanley once again came across Itsi, now somewhat more of a lawless barbarian. Surprisingly, Stanley discovered that, although Frank Pocock was now deceased, the covenant still held. After a time, tension arose between the two men and Stanley suggested that their brotherhood be canceled. "No, no, no," cried Ngalyema anxiously. "Our brotherhood cannot be broken; our blood is now one."

Now for a moment, let us look at a righteous God and sinful man in light of blood covenant relationship. Scripture makes it clear that man had become separated from God. We had lived at such distance that even to come near to him produced antagonism. Our lives were too dissimilar to allow any kind of accord.

Then God comes and says he is willing to make peace with mankind. He is willing to sign a covenant with us. Although God perhaps had established covenants with other men such as Adam and Noah, he eventually comes to a man named

Abram to establish a lasting covenant that would affect all mankind. It would be through this man that all humanity eventually would have the opportunity for a peaceful relationship with God. The accord was to be signed in blood.

God chose the blood of three animals and two birds to ratify the initial part of a two-part treaty. In the first part, God promised to give to Abram's descendants all the land from the Nile River to the Euphrates River and the land of Canaan as an everlasting possession. In the second part, God changed Abram's name to "Abraham" and promised he would make him the father of many nations. God required that Abraham ratify this covenant through the circumcision of every male among his people. This, God said, was the sign of the covenant. It too was a blood covenant. Later this covenant was reestablished with both Isaac and Jacob.

Little did Abraham realize that he was helping to fulfill God's great plan of salvation for all humanity. God wanted to use Abraham's lineage to bring a Savior to earth, One who could deliver mankind from bondage to both sin and Satan.

In the meantime, Abraham's descendants apparently needed specific guidance (a schoolmaster) in order to be preserved from the effects of the bondage they were in. In order that sin, destructive by nature as it is, might not destroy, and so that Satan might not take advantage of them, they needed God's direct protection. Therefore, God was willing to establish a covenant within the covenant he made with Abraham for this protection. It was established with Abraham's descendants, at this time called the children of Israel. The person representing them was Moses.

While the Israelites were moving from Egypt to Canaan, they passed through the Desert of Sinai. It was here God met with them on Mount Sinai to establish this new (Mosaic) covenant. The covenant was to be sealed in blood. Israel was to keep God's laws in exchange for his protection.

"Then he took the Book of the Covenant and read it to the people. They responded, 'We will do everything the Lord has said; we will obey.' Moses then took the blood, sprinkled it on the people and said, 'This is the blood of the covenant that the Lord has made with you in accordance with all these words.' "[1]

But the people soon discovered that they could not keep God's laws. Stubbornness, pride, and selfishness kept them from the simplest of regulations. Since under a blood covenant failure to perform means death, they were doomed.

God's grace, however, provided a remedy. He was willing to have a substitute pay the price of blood so that man would not have to die. As the shedding of blood sealed the covenant, so the shedding of innocent animal blood was to be the price paid to the offended party for breaking the covenant. It was a substitute for the shedding of man's own blood. He had made a covenant with God and had broken it. Both parties knew blood was to be shed.

From the perspective of the New Testament, looking back we see that God would eventually establish a new covenant with all mankind as he carefully fulfilled the Old Covenant with Israel. This New Covenant would allow both Jews and Gentiles to benefit under the original covenant God made with Abraham.

First, the Sinai (Mosaic) Covenant was made only with Israel. It was not made with the other nations of the earth; thus the other nations were not obligated to obey it.

Second, the New Testament is God's New Covenant with any person who, by the blood of Jesus, will enter into it. Those outside of this covenant have no obligation to follow its

demands; nor do they have any right to its protection, blessings, and power.

The Old Testament Covenant at Sinai was finished when
the New Covenant in Christ began. That means that not only
are men outside the current New Covenant relationship not
obligated to its policies but Jews are likewise exempt from
covenant policies because the Old Covenant is no longer in
force.

What does all this mean? A person cannot be saved without
being in covenant relationship with God, but each person
must "cut the covenant" with God himself. And no amount of
personal goodness or good deeds will take the place of such a
relationship.

Christians have no business trying to get those of the world
to live under the conditions of either the Old or the New
Testament. This only frustrates both parties. Our responsibility is to introduce people to covenant relationship with God
through Christ, allowing them to "cut the covenant" themselves. When we are more concerned with how people live
than who they are living for, we are in danger of making
enemies of the Gospel and placing them under the outward
compulsion of keeping the Law in order to become and remain righteous. Simply introduce Christ to men, and he will
clean them up and keep them clean.

Some men serve God legally while others serve him
lovingly.

George D. Watson says:

> Even among the sanctified are two classes, the severe
> and the tender. The severe magnify the legal side of
> holiness, and know but little of that longing desire for
> God that weeps and sighs for His ocean fulness. The
> tender hearted saints magnify personal love for God, get

bright visions of the person and character of God, long
for Him so unutterably that the heart fairly breaks with
sweet, seraphic pain to be lost in the shining abysses of
His glorious being.[2]

Where did the Old Testament end and the New Testament
begin? As Jesus was seated at the Last Supper in the upper
room with the disciples, he took a cup of wine, gave thanks,
and offered it to them, saying, "Drink from it, all of you. This
is my blood of the covenant, which is poured out for many for
the forgiveness of sins."[3] At that moment he "cut the covenant" with them and with any other person who would accept
a relationship with him.

Jesus and his disciples had gathered in that small room to
celebrate the Passover. It would, however, be the last Passover that ever needed to be observed. For as the New Covenant would replace the Old, so the Lord's Supper would
replace the Passover.

Christ is part of both covenants and was fulfilling one (the
old) as he made way for the other (the new). Jesus is the
Passover Lamb anticipated by the Old Testament and the
Maker of a New Covenant signed in his blood. His body
represented the slain lamb necessary for atonement and his
blood the blood of the New Covenant.

When we partake of the cup and the bread of the communion table, we are acknowledging our covenant with Jesus. Our
part of the agreement is that we will live in harmony with him.
His part includes protection, friendship, guidance, and a host
of other blessings. Included within the covenant is his willingness to forgive our sin, based on confession and repentance. His blood shed on the cross guarantees that
forgiveness.[4]

Salvation

Because of the sin that currently affects our race, there is a
break in the relationship which man and God were originally
to enjoy together. God had entered into a trust relationship
with mankind when he created him. Forbidding man to do
certain things in the original Garden seems to be a part of that
accord. The creation of free will produced such individuality
that God needed to have an agreement with man in order to
have fellowship with him. The broken agreement now keeps
us apart, rendering man "lost" from God. Man is away from
God not in the sense that God has misplaced him but in the
sense that he, in his rebellion, has gone astray. Sin has severed his relationship with a holy God. Man has broken the
trust.

The blood of Christ is sufficient substitution to pay for sin
after one is saved by the New Covenant as well as sin before
he was saved.

Should man fail to find his soul and spirit restored to communion with God through covenant relationship, he will continue to remain lost. He will continue to live in a conscious
state of existence forever, but outside of an intimate relationship with his Creator, outside of his intended purpose, and
outside of any kind of real happiness or joy. He will live in a
place where goodness does not exist, a place where the vile,
those who have refused virtue, live together forever. However, let us not forget that God is willing to provide salvation
through blood covenant relationship.

A significant feature of God's salvation process is its current
availability: "Now is the day of salvation."[5] Right now God is
extending an offer for us to be repatriated. He does not want
us to go beyond the door of death without his Spirit living
within us.

Eternal life does not begin after death. It begins now. Jesus, the Creator of all life, is eternal life. *A person can have eternal life only if he has Jesus.*

The wonder of salvation is not found in learning to live by new standards. It is not found by adhering to a set of do's and don'ts, in church membership, or even by witnessing. Salvation comes about solely through inviting Christ to take up residence within the human heart. Paul the Apostle told the people at Colosse that Christ in them was the hope of glory.

What a message Christ within is! Instead of the potential for being demon possessed, we can have the assurance of the indwelling of the Spirit of our Creator—an indwelling designed to help produce inner stability, not one in which God himself brings on another kind of bondage. God does not want to control an individual. He wants to enter our frail frame in order to help us be in control of ourselves.

Christ has come to save us from sin, self-will, and from playing God. Not everyone can be the leader. Not all in a military unit can be the captain. Yet the rebellion we promote suggests such lunacy. Every person wants to be his own god.

In the salvation process, God wants to establish himself as the one true God while he protects man's free will. To do so, he requires that men follow Jesus. "For the Son of Man came to seek and to save what was lost."[6]

Redemption Through Substitution

Make no mistake: sin is at the heart of our broken covenants with God. The horrible abyss of human sinfulness is dug deep into the center of our being, producing self-infatuation. We must not call our broken relationship with God by any name less than that which has caused it: sin.

For God to reestablish a relationship with mankind, someone would first have to pay the price of the broken covenant.

Someone would have to pay to get mankind out of the entanglement that came about because of rebellion and disobedience. Disobedience made us slaves to sin, and the only way out would be through a ransom. A price would have to be paid to secure a release.

The story is told of a little boy who made a boat, put a sail on it, and painted it with happy colors. He tied a string to it and carefully placed it in the water. The wind soon caught the sails and pushed it out into the current, where the force became so strong that it broke the string. The boat headed downstream with the little boy running along the bank after it. He followed the boat, hoping it would come ashore, but finally it went out of sight. Some time later he was in town and happened by an antique store. There in the window display was his little boat with a price tag attached to it. The boy knew that in order to get it back he would have to pay the shopkeeper his price. So he ran home as fast as he could, got all the money out of his piggy bank, and counted out just enough to pay the amount. He went back to the store and purchased his little boat. As he came out the door, he said to the boat, "Twice you are mine. First I made you and now I've bought you." How similar this is to the way God set about to redeem us.

The Old Testament records numerous illustrations of people, property, and livestock set free from bondage by the payment of a price. The firstborn males of all livestock as well as the firstborn males among the Israelites all belonged to the Lord. They could, however, be bought back with a "ransom."

But as is the case in *almost* all things ransomed according to God's requirements, only blood—a life—would be sufficient to pay the price. But why such a high price? And to whom was such a high price to be paid?

In order to understand this price better, let us for a moment consider the subjects of free will and justice.

Free will, originally instilled by God in man as a part of his makeup, was given to assure individuality and to give meaning to a person's choices. For example, for love to be powerful, it must be possible not to love. For righteousness to be a wonderful thing, there must be the ability to choose unrighteousness.

This free will, however, necessitates the condition of moral responsibility. If man wants to be free, he must be responsible. If he won't be responsible, then he can't be free. Freedom is possible only if God is first willing to grant it, and second, if he is willing to protect it. If God pulls back and refuses to protect us because we become irresponsible, we lose our freedom. At this point, both sin and Satan serve to bring us into bondage.

But a man not only loses his freedom when he refuses to be accountable, he is required to pay for the damage he has caused as well. There is no way to grant true free will if there is no guarantee that it will not be violated by the free will of another. Therefore, those who want free will must not misuse it by hurting others. If they do, they must be corrected or punished.

The theology over who was to be paid for the debt incurred by sin has long been a matter of debate among great theologians. Greek writer Origen taught that Christ's death was a price paid to the devil, which is easily disputable since neither God nor man owes him anything. Bishop Ambrose believed it was the "law" that needed satisfaction. But perhaps the best explanation arises from the fact that God remains consistent with himself. That is, he must remain true to his character. It is he who must be satisfied.

It was not God's honor that needed payment. It was God himself. John Stott writes:

> To say that he must "satisfy himself" means that he must be himself and act according to the perfection of his nature or "name." The necessity of "satisfaction" for God, therefore, is not found in anything outside himself but within himself, in his own immutable character. It is an inherent or intrinsic necessity. The law to which he must conform, which he must satisfy, is the law of his own being.[7]

If God were not satisfied, he could not be God. But since he is God, he will be satisfied. Total perfection, which God is, necessitates total satisfaction. Thus the price of sin was paid to God. And the price is high because of the huge amount of damage caused by sin.

So horrible and destructive is the nature of sin that it would take something as drastic and sobering as death itself to pay for its damage. God hates sin, not only because it is in opposition to himself but also because of the pain, suffering, and death it inflicts upon others. But if mankind had to pay the price of a broken covenant with his own blood, the race would soon cease to exist. God was, therefore, willing to accept a substitute. Instead of a man dying for his own sin, a substitute would be found to take his place. The blood that really should be shed—the blood of the offender—could be replaced by other blood. In the Old Testament, the substitute blood was to be that of animals. It would take the death of something innocent, often a lamb, to satisfy the demands of a broken relationship.

But animal blood, as it turned out, was an inadequate substitute for the blood of the offending person. All it served to do was to appease God's anger until something of sufficient value could be substituted.

As a teenager I worked on a ranch where sheep were kept. How cute and lovable they are when they are born, so unlike the creatures they become when they are fully grown. It is hard to imagine what it would be like under the Old Testament to have to go into the flock and select one of these precious and innocent young animals and take it to a priest to be slaughtered, all because I had sinned. This wouldn't happen very many times before I would realize that every time I sinned, someone or something else had to suffer.

Today we are in danger of showing contempt for the blood of Jesus, the blood shed as a substitute for our own. This is easily done by taking sin lightly. How callous we become in regarding sin as something that is "really not all that serious." After all, all we need to do today is tell God we are sorry and he will forgive us. As true as that is, we are in danger of allowing his grace to become a license for sin.

Blood is still the required payment for sin. That will never change. And unless a person has appropriated a blood sacrifice for his sin, he has not been forgiven and God's wrath is not appeased. The unforgiven sinner will, therefore, have to pay the consequences both here on earth in sorrowful reaping and for eternity in hell if he fails to appropriate blood for his sin.

That is why Calvary is so important. Atonement through the cross was needed to satisfy the holiness and justice of God. Mankind was incapable of bringing resolution to the problems he created. Nothing he could do on his own would remedy his separation from God. The only alternative, other than God's redemptive plan, was for man to die for his own sins and be completely discarded in a place where he could do no more damage. That is the place of damnation.

In his love, God sacrificially sought to avoid that possibility.

He was willing to make restitution and to pay the price for sin—the price of blood. The eye-for-an-eye and tooth-for-a-tooth principle was fulfilled in Christ. In unfathomable love he took what we deserved. It was our sin, but he took it. It was our suffering, but he endured it. It was our death, but he accepted it. God was just and demonstrated his tremendous love for us by taking the initiative and becoming the justifier. He offered the blood of his Son as a once-for-all sacrifice to replace the blood of bulls and goats. His blood would be sufficient for all of man's sin, past, present, and future. After acceptance of Christ, when a person sins, Jesus' blood can be applied to cleanse him by simple confession. His sin is then taken away as if it had never happened.

Poet William Cowper so aptly penned these words:

> There is a fountain filled with blood
> Drawn from Emmanuel's veins,
> And sinners plunged beneath that flood
> Lose all their guilty stains.

The marvelous grace of God is not to be seen as a license for sin. God certainly intended for the blood to atone for our daily failures until the fullness of his kingdom comes, but he did not intend for a person to walk knowingly into sin without suffering for it. This is not said to minimize the significance or effectiveness of Christ's blood. It is said to emphasize that we must be very careful concerning the grace of God and must not regard it lightly.

Atonement and Propitiation

In the Old Testament, the shedding of blood not only paid the price of redemption but also served to hide sin from God's eyes and therefore appease his anger.

The word *atonement* means "to cover." Dr. Alfred Cave noted, "The idea expressed by the Hebrew original . . . was cover or covering, not in the sense of rendering invisible to Jehovah, but in the sense of engrossing His sight with something else, of neutralizing sin, so to speak, of disarming it, of rendering it inert to arouse the righteous anger of God."[8]

But does God get angry in such a way that he needs to be propitiated? That is, does his anger need to be pacified or appeased?

To think that God is moody or temperamental and could at any moment fly off the handle at the slightest provocation is a pagan notion. It is counter to his nature to become antagonistic the same way we do. He is never irrational; nor does he ever become revengeful, resentful, spiteful, or vindictive. The idea of God holding a club over the heads of offenders finds no basis in the Word of God. It is a concept that not only lacks biblical foundation but also drastically distorts the true image of God.

How, then, are we to view God's anger? Perhaps one of the best images is that of a judge. Ideally, he holds no prejudice or bias, is not emotionally moved by circumstances, and decides rationally according to established standards.

John Stott writes, "The wrath of God . . . is his steady, unrelenting, unremitting, uncompromising antagonism to evil in all its forms and manifestations. In short, God's anger is poles apart from ours. What provokes our anger (injured vanity) never provokes his; what provokes his anger (evil) seldom provokes ours."[9]

When any covenant is broken, especially a blood covenant, the injured party is likely to become angry, and the guilty party will undoubtedly receive the brunt of the offended person's wrath. Propitiation is therefore necessary. Likewise, God's justice must be satisfied when his anger is aroused by sin. But what will satisfy it? Certainly not the blood of bulls and goats:

> Because it is impossible for the blood of bulls and goats to take away sins. Therefore, when Christ came into the world, he said: "Sacrifice and offering you did not desire, but a body you prepared for me; with burnt offerings and sin offerings you were not pleased. Then I said, 'Here I am—it is written about me in the scroll—I have come to do your will, O God.' " First he said, "Sacrifices and offerings, burnt offerings and sin offerings you did not desire, nor were you pleased with them" (although the law required them to be made). Then he said, "Here I am, I have come to do your will." He sets aside the first to establish the second. And by that will, we have been made holy through the sacrifice of the body of Jesus Christ once for all.[10]

The defilement of something made in the image of God (man) is of such magnitude that only something of at least an equal yet opposite magnitude could result in man's redemption. It would be God himself who would suffer and offer his own blood to be shed in order to pay for man's sin. But since it would take a sacrifice unto death, only a man could shed blood as a price for sin. Mankind's Savior must be a man. "Both the one who makes men holy and those who are made holy are of the same family."[11] "For since death came through a man, the resurrection of the dead comes also through a man."[12] Hence, the God-man Jesus Christ.

Forgiveness and Reconciliation

We have been made with a capacity for spiritual intimacy with God. Not only is this relationship a wonderful privilege; it is also a necessity for full functioning and fulfillment in life.

God made us with a need for a close relationship with himself.

Originally the Spirit of God and the spirit of man enjoyed this wonderful relationship. In the Garden of Eden, God and man walked together in fellowship. But this association was fractured by man's willingness to yield to another who had set himself in opposition to God. Man's capitulation to the Enemy forced God to withdraw. Without God, man was left to his own devices, and as a result we now live in a chaotic world.

Our only hope for restoration is in God's willingness and provision for resuming a relationship with us. But until we are willing to lay down our rebellion and to give up our allegiance to the Enemy, we cannot realize our lost intimacy with God. This restoration of relationship is called reconciliation. It is a coming together again after an estrangement.

The only means God offers for reconciliation is our acceptance of his Son, Jesus Christ. "Christ in you" becomes the only hope for humanity. While on earth, Jesus spoke of this unique plan when he promised to send the Holy Spirit, who would not only walk with an individual but who would literally indwell him as well. There is a Bethlehem manger in each heart awaiting the birth of the King.

The greatest hindrance to reconciliation is still rebellion. It is inherited from Adam and is reinforced by our own desire and by the influence of demon spirits. It is the first thing with which God must deal if we are to be saved. His method of doing so is to introduce only one plan for salvation, and that plan involves his Son, Jesus Christ.

The fact that God offers only one way to himself instantly causes some men to object. Immediately rebellion comes to the surface. Why not Mohammed, or Buddha, or Confucius, or good living? When God says, "No—no one else but Jesus can lead you to me," man's rebellion arises and must be reckoned with.

Some surrender and go God's way. Others do not. Jesus is the dividing line.

What man does with his rebellion is determined by what he does with Jesus Christ. What Jesus wants him to do is to accept him. A. W. Tozer said, "Jesus was born of a virgin, suffered under Pontius Pilate, died on the cross and rose from the grave to make worshipers out of rebels."[13]

The words *forgiveness* and *remission*, sometimes used interchangeably, describe what God does concerning our sins when we accept Christ. *Remission* explains a little better what actually takes place because when we think of forgiveness we may be tempted to think of it in a human sense. Man's forgiveness is often less than complete. True forgiveness causes the offended to bear the full cost of the offense while the offender goes free.

The word *remission* tells us the extent of God's forgiveness in his willingness to pay for our sins. The idea is that sin stops being an issue. In reality it no longer exists. It is looked upon as if it never happened and we are looked upon as if we had not sinned. Note that scars may continue to exist, but sin in terms of its ongoing presence, power, and penalty are gone.

So, under the Old Testament, sins were covered. That is what atonement is all about. Under the New Testament, however, they are not covered; they are remitted. They are put away as though they had never been. And it is the blood of Calvary that remits sin. "But now he has appeared once for all at the end of the ages to do away with sin by the sacrifice of himself."[14]

Performance

The sin in man is more than his propensity for wrongdoing. It is not primarily what he *does* but what he *is* that makes him wrong. He is a sinner programmed to sin, and as long as he continues to deal with sins without first dealing with his *nature* of sin, he will find no solution to his problems. Christ is God's way of helping us, and he has come to change our nature from within.

A great obstacle to salvation is trying to handle one's own sins personally. We are not capable of cleaning up our lives without God's help. He asks that we come to him just as we are, no matter what our problem is. The "just as I am" principle gives God the opportunity to help us.

For some reason, it seems to us much easier to work in order to please God than to be changed by God himself. All such motion toward goodness without God's help is ultimately and eternally meaningless because it simply produces an outward righteousness which disguises inward vileness. As long as the accomplishment comes from an outward command and not an inward motivation, the endeavor produces only dead religion, and God is not honored.

The Old Testament Law did two things: First, it showed man the kind of righteousness necessary in order to please God. Second, it proved the total impossibility of man, in his fallen condition, to obey God. Sooner or later, the best law-keeper failed. And if he offended on one point, he was guilty of breaking the whole law. Man would need help from God if he were to be obedient. He would need to become a new creation, and that could be accomplished only through Jesus Christ.

Jesus Christ has become a stumbling block to many because God insists that he be the only mediator between God and man.

Even if we do accept Christ, we often stumble at grace as a free gift. *Certainly,* we think, *there must be something I can do to pay for it.* And even after he insists that there isn't, we still endeavor to earn it.

Why is it so hard to accept this love of God without feeling obligated to pay for it? Why is it so hard to let love be the means of motivation to dedication and service? Why do we insist on man-made rules and regulations to establish our worthiness? It is so hard to just say, "Thank you."

Part 2

In the day and age in which Jesus lived, punishments for crimes worthy of death often were carried out by crucifixion. Death was slow and painful to individuals who were either tied or nailed to large wooden posts sunk deep into the ground.

Although leaders of the Jewish people sought to end the life of Christ, they had no legal right to put any man to death. All such punishment fell under the authority of the Roman government. Therefore, they sought to influence government officials to have him crucified.

After his arrest in the Garden and his appearance before the religious Jews, Jesus was sent to Pilate, the Roman governor, for trial. But Pilate found nothing in him worthy of death. Pilate's vain attempt to convince the people that Jesus should be turned loose was met only by opposition that accused him of promoting a king other than Caesar. Pilate feared both Jesus and the Jews as well as Caesar. Pressure from the crowd soon won out, and Pilate allowed them to take Christ to be crucified.

Pilate was deeply touched by his encounter with Jesus. He sensed something different about him and may have even suspected he was the Son of God. He was eager to make it known that he had not initiated Christ's condemnation. He stated his belief in Jesus' innocence to the crowd and before them he washed his hands, symbolically affirming his separation from anything to do with Christ's crucifixion. Later, still concerned about the matter, he had a sign prepared and fastened to the cross. It read, "Jesus of Nazareth, the King of the Jews." When the chief priests protested, "Do not write 'The King of the Jews,' but that this man claimed to be the king of the Jews," Pilate answered, "What I have written, I have written."[15]

All of the events now unfolding were not accidents; nor were they afterthoughts of God. These things had been clearly seen in his wisdom from the "creation of the world."[16] Every step of Christ toward the cross appears downward, but every step out of and away from the tomb is upward. "Therefore God exalted him to the highest place."[17]

Father, Forgive Them

As Jesus stood near the cross to which he would shortly be fastened with large nails driven through his hands and feet and then into the wood, he was offered a drink of wine mixed with gall. Perhaps it was a stupefying mixture to help relieve some of the pain. As soon as Jesus tasted it, he refused it. He was facing a battle in which he needed all of his faculties. Nothing must dim his senses if he were to finish the task at hand.

As each blow of the hammer drove the nails to their destination, could he think of anything but the reason this was happening? He had come to rescue lost humanity, and it would require the sacrifice of himself to do so.

In the midst of strong emotions venting themselves all around him, Jesus uttered some remarkable words. They were words not expected from men about to die at the cruel hands of others: "Father, forgive them, for they do not know what they are doing."[18] Did such a prayer concern only those soldiers ignorantly doing the Enemy's work? Was it a prayer to forestall the armies of heaven from immediately responding and striking these men dead? Or was it a prayer for all mankind?

Most certainly it was not a blanket pardon for these men or for the world at large. Divine love will never force itself on human free will. If men are not interested in forgiveness through repentance, God will not insist they receive it. The "if any man" invitation from the knock on the heart's door is to continue the guarantee that God will not demand service to himself against our will. No doubt God was saying, "Forgive this act done in ignorance." But he certainly was not praying that the sins of man in general be forgiven. Only repentance and faith in him would take care of the immense problem of the nature of sin.

We must also acknowledge that it was not a universal pardon for man's ignorance. Among other things, ignorance carries a curious blend of intuition, which tells us we should have known better, and a vacuum of factual input. The sins of carelessness and neglect mix adversely with understanding to produce a denseness for which we want to be considered blameless. But God does not hold a casual attitude toward sin. Sin is serious business with him. He does, however, extend forgiveness to those who sincerely want and seek it.

If his prayer was not directed primarily at stopping heaven's angels from intervening, it no doubt did that as a by-product. It is hard to imagine that they would withhold an invasion without being commanded to do so.

The soldiers responsible for crucifying Jesus wanted his clothes and set about dividing them among themselves. One of the garments was seamless, woven in one piece from top to bottom. Not wanting to tear it, they decided to cast lots for it, fulfilling the Scripture that says, "They divided my garments among them and cast lots for my clothing."[19]

I Tell You the Truth

As Jesus hung there in open shame, one of the thieves hanging close by insulted him: "Aren't you the Christ? Save yourself and us!" The other criminal, however, rebuked the first, saying, "Don't you fear God since you are under the same sentence? We are punished justly, for we are getting what our deeds deserve. But this man has done nothing wrong." He then turned to Jesus and said, "Jesus, remember me when you come into your kingdom." Jesus answered, "I tell you the truth, today you will be with me in paradise."[20]

Russell Jones comments:

> At this point in the tragic drama something happened that struck the death-blow to some of the most dangerous and persistent heresies of the ages. In the salvation of one of the thieves, vital theology finds one of its finest demonstrations. Sacramentalism was refuted, for the thief was saved without recourse to baptism, the Lord's Supper, church, ceremony, or good works.
>
> The dogma of purgatory was refuted, for this vile sinner was instantly transformed into a saint and made fit for paradise apart from his personal expiation of a single sin.
>
> The teaching of universalism was refuted, for only one was saved of all who might have been saved. Jesus did not say, "To day ye shall be with me in paradise," but "To day thou shalt be with me in paradise."
>
> The notion of soul sleep was refuted, for the clear implication of the entire incident is that the redeemed thief would be in conscious fellowship with his Saviour

in paradise even while his body disintegrated in some grave.

Too, it is doubtful whether any gospel incident presents the plan of salvation more clearly and simply.[21]

From about noon until 3:00 P.M. the sun ceased to shine and darkness covered the land. The temple veil, which some believe was several inches thick, was strangely yet powerfully torn in two, not from bottom to top as one might assume if it had been done by human hands, but as God would do it, from top to bottom, signifying that there was now nothing separating man from God.

Dear Woman

Who else but a mother can know a mother's love? And who can know a mother's pain at the loss of a child except the mother of that child? As Mary watched her firstborn hanging between heaven and earth, her heart was wrenched in agony. The words of Simeon were being fulfilled in that "a sword will pierce your own soul too."[22]

Perhaps Mary remembered many of the details of his life: the manger, his first steps, his work as a carpenter, the time he became separated from the family on the long journey to the temple, and the early days of his ministry. She no doubt remembered the angel's first visit and the times she wondered what it was all about. In spite of what Simeon had said, how could she ever have imagined this?

The beginning of Jesus' ministry brought the beginning of the end of the earthly mother-son relationship between him and Mary. At the wedding in Cana, where he turned water into wine, he used the word *woman* rather than *mother* in addressing Mary. Later, when it was reported that his mother and brothers had come to see him, he asked, "Who are my mother and my brothers?"[23] Jesus had not rejected them but was simply putting a different perspective on his relationship with them.

Mary was losing her son. She was no longer to be his mother. Little did she realize, however, that she was about to gain a Savior. As her son was slowly slipping away, her God was steadily approaching. What appears to be almost a harshness in Jesus is a love that sought to have Mary release her claim on him as her son so that she might lay claim to him as her God.

Edmund Schlink wrote, "God is not in Jesus because Jesus is the Son of Mary. But God in His complete independence of man determined to become man through Mary, and He remains God. It is not the son of Mary who is the Son of God, but it is the Son of God who became the Son of Mary! He is much more than her Son. Jesus is the Savior in that He is the Word of God who became flesh."[24]

When Jesus said to Mary, "Dear woman, here is your son," speaking of John and not of himself, and then to John, "Here is your mother," he broke forever the chords that maintained their earthly relationship.[25] It was not "Dear mother," it was "Dear woman," and it was meant to end one bond as he established another.

His words were not as painful as one might think. The word *woman* here is the Greek word *gunai* and carries the attitude of endearing respect. It has none of the harshness that may be implied by modern usage. Regardless, these were not easy words because they still spoke of separation. But no doubt something in Mary's heart bore witness that they were necessary words. It is much easier to bear loss when there is hope that something better is to be gained.

Jesus might have been concerned that Mary's initial responsibility of bearing him not be construed as more than it was.

Now she was to be numbered among the disciples of the ages. Her role would not be that of a mediator between God and man. She would hold no claim to possessing God.

There might already have been a subtle attempt by the Enemy to detract from Christ's ministry as mediator when a woman exclaimed, "Blessed is the mother who gave you birth and nursed you." Jesus was quick to reply, "Blessed rather are those who hear the word of God and obey it" (Luke 11:27, 28). He immediately shifted the emphasis away from Mary because her ministry had been completed and any exaltation of her would only detract from the Gospel message.

Jesus was ever vitally concerned that the Law be properly fulfilled. Through John, whom he knew he could trust, he provided for the future welfare of his mother. No one could ever accuse him of dishonoring father or mother according to the Law of Moses. Providing for Mary's needs when he could no longer personally do so was a profound act of love which served all the more to fulfill the Law.

My God, My God

At about noon on the day of the Crucifixion, a strange darkness covered the land. Three hours later, Jesus cried out in a loud voice, "My God, my God, why have you forsaken me?"[26]

Perhaps no other saying of Jesus is more difficult to understand than this one. It is reported that Martin Luther once gave himself to intense meditation trying to understand the meaning to these words. He finally rose to exclaim, "God forsaken of God! Who can understand that?" Again, the thought of God and the thought of suffering are at such complete odds with each other that to suggest God suffered would appear to be a contradiction of such profound proportion that the statement might be rendered the ultimate blasphemy.

Disunity in the Godhead, yet perfect unity at the same time? Separation, yet perfect oneness? The appearance seems not only blasphemous but absurd as well. Regardless, salvation for mankind finds its greatest wonder in the fact that God *did* suffer.

Writing to the Philippians, Paul explained what was happening in what appeared to be the bleakest moment in human history. Speaking of Jesus, Paul wrote, "Who, being in very nature God, did not consider equality with God something to be grasped, but made himself nothing, taking the very nature of a servant, being made in human likeness."[27]

To be made in human likeness in every way, Christ would have to experience all the experiences of humanity. He would have to know what it was like to suffer. He would need to know sorrow. Worst of all, like us, he would have to experience separation from God. It wasn't until he took upon himself the sins of the world that he became alienated from God like every other man. The only difference was that he had never sinned. Physical pain—the nails; emotional pain—the severed relationship with his mother and brothers; and now spiritual pain—estrangement from his Father, would cause him to understand every basic problem man would ever face.

Many afflictions touch our lives, but few are as terrible as loneliness. No pain seems to go so deep as when no one else is there. An empty house, meals for one, and silence—deafening silence.

Days before the Crucifixion, Jesus had cried to the Father and had received comforting words. Now, heaven was silent. Why? Because he was made "to be sin for us, so that in him we might become the righteousness of God."[28] Jesus became like us that we might become like him.

God cannot and will not abide sin. It is so inconsistent with his nature that he must do something about it. But it is only to the person who will cry, "My God, my God," that he will turn his attention.

Here, in the face of unfathomable suffering, Jesus' cry to the Father was met with unfathomable grace that brought him through to victory over our sin. Before Jesus stormed the gates of hell, he stormed the gates of grace, crying, "My God." God's answer to his cry was redemption for you and me.

I Am Thirsty

"Later, knowing that all was now completed, and so that the Scripture would be fulfilled, Jesus said, 'I am thirsty.' "[29] Generally, when a person is thirsty he will ask for something specific, such as water. But Jesus did not ask for a drink; he simply stated a condition so the Scriptures could be fulfilled. Although his physical body was now crying out desperately in pain, he was more concerned that every prophecy be fulfilled completely so that there would be no possibility of questioning his authenticity. Carefully he formed the words, "I am thirsty." Immediately a sponge soaked with wine vinegar on the end of a hyssop plant was extended to him, thus fulfilling Psalm 69:20, 21: "I looked for sympathy, but there was none, for comforters, but I found none. They put gall in my food and gave me vinegar for my thirst."

It Is Finished

"When he had received the drink, Jesus said, 'It is finished.' "[30] What was finished? The plan of salvation was finished. Jesus' work of reconciliation was done. All he had left to do was to rise from the dead and ascend to be with the Father, and the plan for rescuing mankind would be fully in place. Christ had met every condition for bringing mankind back into a relationship with the Father. He had struck the death blow that eventually would destroy all the works of the

Enemy. His shed blood had met the conditions necessary for satisfying universal and eternal jurisprudence. His blood was sufficient to pay the penalty for man's sin. The sacrifice was complete.

The spectacle of death no longer draws attention. The jeering crowd is mostly gone. Their hate-filled excitement and agitation has lost its fervency. The thieves hanging next to Jesus are no doubt silent, except perhaps for an occasional moan. A few people stand nearby but can no longer look upon his pain. Soldiers remain only out of duty. As far as everyone is concerned, the Crucifixion is over. But it isn't this event that Christ speaks of as being finished. It is his mission to earth. He did not give up. He won a decisive victory for mankind. He overcame. He succeeded. Salvation for mankind was complete.

He did not die a martyr or an idealist. He died the substitute, the sacrifice. His death was not an accident or a mistake. His death was a finished work.

Edmund Schlink wrote:

> The heavenly Father is now free to love lost men into His eternal Kingdom without violating His holy justice. Man, by his sin, had put himself outside the realm of God's saving love but inside the jurisdiction of His condemning justice. But now, the eternal Son, by His substitution, had carried God's love into man's realm of rebellion, satisfied the demands of God's justice, and invited man to come back home to God and love. Since Jesus paid the price of human redemption with His own precious blood, God can now receive the repenting, returning sinner both as a loving Father and as a just God.[31]

Father, Into Your Hands I Commit My Spirit

This was the climax of Jesus' life on earth. These were his final words—and what wonderful words they are. They were spoken with assurance because he knew he had pleased the Father. Not many people die confident of having done all to please God and of having lived well among other people. Certainly none do it perfectly as this man did. And sadly, some do nothing to please God.

Thomas Hobbs, a skeptic who influenced some of the great men of England, said before he died, "If I had the whole world, I would give it to live one day. I am about to take a leap into the dark!" Napoleon Bonaparte moaned, "I die before my time, and my body will be given to the earth. Such is the fate of him who has been called the great Napoleon. What an abyss between my deep misery and the eternal kingdom of Christ!" Voltaire, the French infidel, said to his doctor, "I am abandoned by God and man! I will give you half of what I am worth if you will give me six months' life. Then I shall go to hell; and you will go with me. O Christ! O Jesus Christ!" John Wilkes Booth, who assassinated President Lincoln, lamented, "Useless! Useless!" How different are the words of these from those who have known the Master.

Charles Wesley said, "I shall be satisfied with thy likeness. Satisfied." John Bunyan: "Weep not for me, but for yourselves. I go to the Father of our Lord Jesus Christ; where I hope we shall ere long meet to sing the new song and remain happy forever; world without end. Amen!" John Calvin: "Thou, Lord, bruisest me, but I am abundantly satisfied, since it is from thy hand."

In his last words, Christ placed himself and all he had done fully into the Father's hand. He had been committed with the responsibility of reconciling men to God and had finished his responsibility. Soon he would be seated next to the Father so that all who come to him at the bidding of the Holy Spirit would find him waiting joyfully.

In the words of Herschel Hobbs, "May we not, then, infer

that we have in Jesus' seventh word from the cross the filing of His report as to the completion of His task? Thus the Captain of our salvation reports to His Commander-in-Chief the successful completion of the assignment. The enemy has been defeated. Satan's forces are routed. And King Jesus is in control of the battlefield."[32]

10
Crucified With Christ

The Apostle Paul was so moved by the cross and so in love with Christ that in his desire for identification with him he said, "For I resolved to know nothing while I was with you except Jesus Christ and him crucified."[1]

Oswald Chambers said, "His Cross is the door by which every member of the human race can enter into the life of God; by His resurrection He has the right to give eternal life to any man, and by His Ascension Our Lord enters heaven and keeps the door open for humanity."[2]

Dr. F. J. Huegel offered, "The world's throne is a cross. Christ reigns from the tree."

No person can fully anticipate the road he will travel once Jesus has said to him, "Come follow me," and we respond by laying down our rebellion. We are eager to work. We would like to make our mark in the world for the Lord. It isn't long, however, before we begin to wonder if we haven't gotten our marching orders confused. The New Birth was glorious, but it was not without pain. We've done just enough ministry to know we can't do it by ourselves. And Gethsemane—we have sometimes wrestled with the Lord until we were exhausted. Could there possibly be more? Yes, much more.

As the cross was the point of victory for Jesus, the cross life for the believer will also result in conquest. But for some reason I shiver at the thought. I then realize I have not spent sufficient time in Gethsemane to know what will happen on the cross. Gethsemane convinces me that the cross will do me no harm, for what must die was of no value in the first place.

The Cross Life

In his first epistle, Peter noted an aspect of the life that God has called us to live in Jesus. "Christ," he said, "suffered for you, leaving you an example, that you should follow in his steps."[3]

John wrote something similar: "This is how we know what love is: Jesus Christ laid down his life for us. And we ought to lay down our lives for our brothers."[4]

Few subjects in Christian life cause as much confusion as the subject of the cross. The same forboding sky that cast its pall over Golgotha broods ominously in the heavens above us as we cast a glance at the cross. The tempest and the earthquake pour out their fury in our hearts so that we dare not even look at its shadow. The cross suggests pain, and we don't like pain. But if the cross is going to have more than a historical significance, it must be transferred in its entirety into the life of the believer.

Paul Rees tells this story: "Two ministers were gazing, raptured, upon the glories of an autumn scene. Said one,

'Behold the sorrows of summer.' 'What do you mean by that?' inquired the other. Replied the first, 'When life is at its richest and best, something or somebody is paying a terrible price.' He was right. Death is ever the price of life."[5]

The cross seems wonderful as a way of remembering the victory of Calvary, but sadly so few see it as a place where self-pity, self-justification, resentment, jealousy, hatred, bitterness, pride, and all the other works of the flesh are to die. And as Saint Augustine said, the cross passed from the scene of public executions to the diadem of the Caesars, and the downgrade movement began.[6]

"The cross of Christ," said Dean Stanley, "is the pledge to us that the deepest suffering may be the condition of highest blessing."

Both from Scripture and from an inner intuitive sense we know that something within us is repugnant to God, something that must be eliminated, something that must be taken to the cross if we are to have a congenial relationship with the Lord. The difficulty arises from trying to identify that *something*. We tend to think it is something very dear to us and that losing it will take away our identity, our specialness. To give it up, then, will be very painful. Nothing could be further from the truth. Of course, there is pain involved. But it is similar to the antiseptic a doctor applies to fight infection. It stings, but it is much better than the pain of amputation.

But the more pain we see in a cross, the more we look at that sacred hill, and the more its radiance shines. And wherever its brilliance enters—our homes, churches, communities, marriages—it leaves a remarkable richness that comforts our sorrows and enhances our joys. The wonder of his cross must be allowed to alert us to the glories of the crosses we are asked to bear.

For the believer, the cross deals with two elements: the first is our "old nature." This is basically the mind-set we have as a result of Adam's fall and the continuous influence of the Satanic forces in the world. Since Satan has the complete destruction of the human race in mind, he has endeavored to set into human thinking a vileness that causes us to self-destruct. The sordid, corrupt, and base way in which many people live was introduced to them as a suggestion for fulfill-ment or as a way to truly enjoy life. But such living produces the opposite results.

What must be destroyed, then, is the old way of thinking, and this must be replaced with a new nature. This is all accomplished when Christ, by his Spirit, is invited to take up residence within us. "I have been crucified with Christ and I no longer live, but Christ lives in me."[7] "For we know that our old self was crucified with him so that the body of sin might be done away with, that we should no longer be slaves to sin—because anyone who has died has been freed from sin."[8]

We must never assume that conversion is simply obeying commands. It is much more than outward performance. It is allowing our very nature to be changed so that from the heart we are participants in the things of God.

After man had partaken of the Tree of the Knowledge of Good and Evil, he was driven from the Garden so that he would not be allowed to take and eat from the Tree of Life and live forever. Perhaps God saw that man, in his willingness to be corrupted and influenced by the Enemy, would receive the wonderful blessings of the Lord by eating of this tree, but at the same time he would be filled with a selfish and sinful heart. The King's inner court is not for the uncommitted, the unfaithful, and the disobedient.

There is something else within, even after conversion, that has the potential to destroy us if we do not guard against it.

Paul the Apostle calls it the "flesh." Sometimes Christians call it "self," a poor definition unless adequately explained. We might also call it the "sinful nature"—not "old nature," for that is done away with in Christ. This thing called the flesh is the second thing that is to be nailed to the cross. Whereas the crucifixion of the old nature is a one-time event, the flesh must be offered up daily.

In order to deal properly with these things, we must first understand what they are. The flesh is basically our body senses exerting influence over our spirit. Considering our makeup—body, soul, and spirit—it is important to recognize that our soul stands between our body and spirit, giving heed to the body (creating flesh) or to the spirit (creating spiritual man). "This I say then, Walk in the Spirit, and ye shall not fulfil the lust of the flesh."[9] Our will, which is a part of the soul, becomes responsible for determining which direction we take.

The Spirit of God gives the soul and spirit the ability to cooperate so that the body does not overexert itself to the point of impinging upon their functions, thus creating sin. Of course, the senses, impulses, and instincts of the body are not wrong in and of themselves. They become wrong when we seek to fulfill them to the point of neglecting the soul and spirit. When we care for nothing but the functions of the body, we perform in much the same way animals do. How often do we say that a person is "proud as a peacock," "stubborn as a mule," "sly as a fox," or that he "eats like a horse" or "has the manners of a pig."

Crucifying the Flesh

Before Christ ever went to the cross, he spoke of the place of a cross in the life of a believer: "If anyone would come after me, he must deny himself and take up his cross and follow me."[10] The implication was that a person was to die to his sinful nature and anything else that prevented the kingdom of God from being established in his life. It wasn't until Jesus had ascended to the Father and we realized what the fullness of salvation was all about that mankind recognized his need for daily cross experiences. The cross the believer has been asked to carry is more than what happens at salvation. It is a life-style that deals daily with the flesh, that part of us that is taken up by pleasing our own minds, emotions, and bodily senses to the exclusion of our spiritual needs and the needs of others.

After our "old nature" is put to death in the cross of Christ, we need to deal with our flesh every day. No other procedure guarantees fellowship with God. When the Apostle Paul said, "I have been crucified with Christ and I no longer live, but Christ lives in me," he was acknowledging that in Christ his old life (nature) had ceased to exist. The life that he was now living was a new life formed by the new nature of Christ. But he was still obligated to put his flesh in its proper place. And he was assured the ability to do so by the power of the indwelling Christ. All God needed was for him to be willing and then to ask for help.

Paul relates a troubling experience no doubt designed to lead him into a life of dying to the flesh. In order that he might be kept from conceit, he was given a "thorn" in the flesh, a messenger of Satan to torment him. Exactly what problem he faced is not mentioned. All we know is that God refused to take it away. Since it is referred to as a problem in his flesh, we must assume it was something that pulled him toward wanting to please his body in a way that was potentially unhealthy to his spiritual life.

Evidently the thorn was allowed to remain in order to cause

Paul to see his weakness and in response turn to Christ as his source of strength. Such an approach to overcoming caused Paul to say, "I delight in weaknesses, in insults, in hardships, in persecutions, in difficulties. For when I am weak, then I am strong."[11]

Thorns in the flesh are not joyful. They are personal, painful, and often persistent. But they usually serve some purpose. They frequently rebuke, refine, restore, restructure, and renew. And in the process we are humbled. We learn to trust God. We experience his grace and power, and eventually God is glorified.

But thorns are often different from crosses, and although there is some dying that takes place in both cases, the difference is significant. Thorns may get our attention in such a way as to lead us to crosses, but they are not the same.

What are crosses? Basically, they are life situations, usually very difficult, that are to be chosen because they are the right things to do. They are the things that could be neglected or shunned for some other personal gratification but are not because of potential pain to others. They are a willingness to suffer so that someone else will not. A parent may give up a vacation so a child can go to camp. An individual may elect to teach Sunday school to affect the lives of others, giving up attending a class for his or her own benefit. Money for new shoes or a new coat may be given because of a missionary need. All these represent some sort of self-sacrifice that could be avoided if desired.

Crosses must be chosen; they are never forced upon a person. On the other hand, thorns come whether we want them or not. Crosses are for obedience. Thorns correct, chasten, and reprove. Crosses require right choices; thorns require a right attitude.

Let me illustrate further. At times a Christian may feel

obligated to be honest in his work situation when an employer expects him to lie for the company. Such decisions sometimes result in termination. Choosing honesty may lead to a cross. The thorn is the temptation toward dishonesty and the problem of dealing with the situation. The cross is the result of a decision to do right. The process of choosing is Gethsemane.

At other times we may face illness, financial loss, or even the death of a loved one. These usually do not represent crosses. Rather they are either thorns themselves, or they produce thorns. Our right choices in response to these situations are the crosses.

Choosing the Cross

The power of the believer's cross will remain greatly ineffective unless we fully understand what the cross means. We must see first that it deals with our selfish goals as they revolve around the flesh: the "I," "me," and "mine" of life that is unconcerned about the welfare of others. The cross moves us to a right relationship with God, others, and ourselves.

Next we must understand that crosses have a direct correlation to our will. In other words, crosses always result as a matter of choice. God has given us free will, which means we have the ability to do bad things as well as good things. We can choose to walk after the flesh or we can choose to walk after the spirit. It is difficult to imagine a kind of free will that could make only one choice. If it could choose only good, it would be a limited free will, and such limitation would mean it was not truly free.

When someone loves us, we usually want him or her to do so because that is their will and not because they are forced. Robots serve little to provide intimacy because their every move is programmed. There can be no real fellowship with them.

A Deeper Death

Most people will agree that putting away all things which are sinful constitutes dying to self. The cross, however, often demands that we go beyond the sinful things of life and learn to die even to some things that may be legitimate—things that, although they are not sinful, could hinder our usefulness in the kingdom.

George D. Watson wrote:

> There are a number of things which are not sinful, nevertheless our attachment to them prevents our greatest fulness of the Holy Spirit and our amplest cooperation with God. Infinite wisdom takes us in hand, and arranges to lead us through deep, interior crucifixion to our fine parts, our lofty reason, our brightest hopes, our cherished affections, our religious views, our dearest friendship, our pious zeal, our spiritual impetuosity, our spiritual arrogance, our narrow culture, our creed and churchism, our success, our religious experiences, our spiritual comforts; the crucifixion goes on till we are dead and detached from all creatures, all saints, all thoughts, all hopes, all plans, all tender heart yearnings, all preferences; dead to all troubles, comforts or annoyances; dead to all climates and nationalities; dead to all desire but for Himself.[12]

Paul Billheimer offers some further insights into the cross life:

> It is of little use for us to talk about being ready to die for Christ while we refuse to submit to the cross as it slays

our self-life in the endless varieties of daily living. The soul that is truly decentralized accepts all that comes to it of pain or sorrow, of disappointment or slight, of misunderstanding or misconception, as an opportunity to die more deeply to the central ego which would contest Christ's sole authority over it. The only question the truly decentralized soul will ask is not "How is this thing going to affect my interests?" but "How is it going to affect Christ's glory?" My feelings, my prerogatives, my comfort, my taste, none of these count. All that matters is that Christ shall be magnified, "whether by life or by death."[13]

Death to the self-life is never an easy matter. Once a person makes the commitment to take up his cross, he is in for a real battle. Jeers and taunts frequently will tempt him to come down from the cross and save himself. Satan will put everything possible in his path to deter him from his abandonment to self, and from his quest for sanctification. And just as Christ could have come down from the cross, so can the believer. Only love held Christ to the cross. Only love will hold us there as well.

An unknown writer helps us understand a little better what it means to "die to self":

1. When you are forgotten or neglected or purposely set at naught, and you don't sting and hurt with the insult or the oversight, but your heart is happy, being counted worthy to suffer for Christ, that is dying to self.

2. When your good is evil spoken of, when your wishes are crossed, your advice disregarded, your opinions ridiculed, and you refuse to let anger rise in your heart, or even defend yourself, but take it all in patient, loving silence, that is dying to self.

3. When you are content with any food, any raiment, any

climate, any society, any solitude, any interruption by the will of God, that is dying to self.

4. When you never care to refer to yourself in conversation, or record your own good works, or itch after commendation, when you truly love to be unknown, that is dying to self.

5. When you can see your brother prosper and have his needs met, and can honestly rejoice with him in spirit and feel no envy or question God, though your own needs are far greater and you are in desperate circumstances, that is dying to self.

6. When you can receive correction and reproof from someone of less stature than yourself, and can humbly submit inwardly as well as outwardly, finding no resentment or rebellion rising up in your heart, that is dying to self.

Forgiving and Forgiveness Because of the Cross

Much has been said of late about forgiveness, some of it perhaps a little erroneous. The general thought is that forgiveness needs to be unconditional. But can we look at forgiveness this way in light of the cross? A wrong view of interpersonal forgiveness corrupts our view of God's forgiveness.

Does God forgive unconditionally? The answer is definitely and scripturally "No!" He surely loves unconditionally, but he forgives only on the basis of repentance. Is God asking man to be more generous than himself? Is God asking man to do something he will not do himself? Or is this simply man's teaching?

Forgiveness is one of the major steps necessary for reconciliation and restoration of damaged relationships. But the first step in the process must be repentance. Jesus taught that we were to forgive to the number "seventy times seven" the people who offend us. But he also taught that such forgiveness was to be on the basis of "If he listens to you, to two or three witnesses, or to the Church." In other words, there needed to be repentance. He went on to say, "If he refuses to listen . . . treat him as you would a pagan or a tax collector."[14]

God looks at man with unconditional love, not unconditional forgiveness. These are not the same concepts and must not be confused. Until the necessary repentance takes place we can, however, make a commitment to God by saying we stand *ready* to forgive. That is, in our hearts we have forgiven and harbor no hatred, animosity, or ill will against those who have offended us. An attitude that says, "I am ready for reconciliation," may put the offending party much more at ease in coming for pardon.

We must also recognize that God loves *us* unconditionally but forgives us only on the basis of repentance. Jesus said, "But unless you repent, you too will all perish."[15]

They Were Expendable

When I was about twelve years old, I read a book called *They Were Expendable.* It described vividly the heroism of men who went off to war knowing they faced the possibility of death. I read with great interest how they endured incredible hardships for their country. They were so dedicated to the cause of freedom that they were willing to expend their lives to protect it.

When we consider the dedication it took some men to accomplish the tasks they set out to do, we may be tempted to wonder why it is that Christianity today so lacks that kind of commitment.

Winston Churchill called for patriots and promised them only blood, toil, sweat, and tears.

Napoleon's soldiers rallied around him when he addressed them with the hope of only more struggle: "You have gained battles without cannon, passed rivers without bridges, performed forced marches without shoes, bivouacked without strong liquors and often without bread. Thanks for your perseverance! But soldiers, you have done nothing—there remains much to do!"

Italy had a liberator named Garibaldi. He said, "I am going out from Rome. I offer neither pay, nor quarters, nor provisions; I offer hunger, thirst, forced marches, battles, death. Let him who loves his country in his heart and not with his lips only, follow me."

I have often heard of the dedication of Communists. Many consider the pleasures of life, personal aspirations, and their very lives expendable for the cause.

Why is it that Christianity seems to shy away from such dedication? Why do we sometimes put a greater emphasis on prosperity than on self-sacrifice? Could it be that we are not aware a war is going on? Perhaps we are slow to believe that Christ came to this earth on a rescue mission. Maybe if we really understood the colossal war going on all about us over the souls of men, we would be more inclined to offer ourselves as expendable.

Trusting Because of the Cross

Repeated cross experiences bring God's blessing and reality into our lives, and his presence draws us into a trust relationship with himself. And God *does* ask us to trust him, although that can be difficult at times. Moses constantly felt the weight of doubting Israel when they were put to the test time and again while coming out of Egypt.

Zechariah did not believe the angel when he foretold of the

birth of his son, John. Mary and Martha doubted that anything could be done for Lazarus after he lay in the tomb for
several days. Thomas questioned if Christ had truly risen
from the dead. We need the utmost faith and concentration to
believe that God can and will do what he says he will do. But
when we see how much faith we really have, compared to how
much we need, we panic. It is here that God is faithful and
willing to impart his faith to us. The writer of the Book of Acts
spoke of "the faith that comes through him."[16] Paul wrote to
the Galatians about the "faith in the Son of God."[17] To the
Ephesians he wrote concerning the "faith in him."[18] It is his
faith, increasingly imparted to us as we remain faithful, that
makes us strong.

Suppose you are totally worn out. Your faith seems gone.
There appears to be no strength in you. Do you realize that
God's storehouse contains faith as much as any other blessing
and that you can stand and call to him for help? Is he too
weak, too frail, to open the windows of heaven and shower
down a blessing on you?

Doubt may hinder your progress as you move through cross
experiences toward the throne of God, but only unbelief can
really stop you. Continue on, weary soldier. Call on him frequently. Realize that he is not just mighty but Almighty as
well as all-knowing, all-wise, all-present, and all-merciful.
Trust him in the darkness as well as in the light.

William Gurnall wrote:

> There are times when a saint is called to trust in a with-
> drawing God. "[Let him] that walketh in darkness and
> hath no light . . . trust in the name of the Lord" (Isa.
> 50:10). This requires a bold step of faith—to venture
> into God's presence with the same temerity as Esther
> into Ahasuerus's presence. Even when no smile lights

His face, when no golden scepter is extended to summon us to come near, we must press forward with this noble resolution: "If I perish, I perish" (Esther 4:16).

Which leads our faith one step further: We must trust also in a "killing God." We must declare with Job, "Though he slay me, yet will I trust in him" (Job 13:15). It takes a submissive faith for a soul to march steadily forward while God seems to fire upon that soul and shoot His frowns like poisoned arrows into it. This is hard work, and will test the Christian's mettle. Yet such a spirit we find in the poor woman of Canaan, who caught the bullets Christ shot at her, and with a humble boldness sent them back again in her prayer (Matt. 15:22–28).[19]

Thus we find that upon choosing the cross life there are certain difficulties we could have avoided if we had chosen to do so. But regardless of the immediate trials we are suffering in order to fulfill righteousness, we soon discover that in the end we have escaped other more serious problems.

Are you tempted to complain about the thorns of life that are common to all people, calling them crosses and becoming angry with God because they are there? Or do you realize that certain problems exist because of the condition of our world and that other problems, such as persecution, have come our way because we have *chosen* the cross?

❈11❈
The Resurrection of Jesus Christ

After the stone had been rolled across the entrance to the tomb, there remained little but the quiet resolve that it was all over.

"Something went wrong."

"I don't understand!"

"How can this be?"

"We had hoped that he was the one who was going to redeem Israel."[1]

Things certainly did not turn out as expected. High hopes now lay shattered, like so many pieces of broken pottery. So complete was the devastation that Jesus' followers began to walk away in defeat. Sadly they made plans to return to their former life-styles. There was little excitement as fishermen considered their nets and businessmen their previous trades. But as quiet as everything seemed on the surface, the violence of hell itself had been invaded, and in a matter of a few days a conquering King would step forth.

Guards had been posted at the tomb to assure that the body of Jesus would not be stolen by his disciples in order for them to claim that he had risen from the dead.

Early in the morning of the third day after Jesus' burial, there was a violent earthquake. An angel whose appearance was like lightning and whose clothes were as white as snow came and rolled the stone away and sat on it.

It is difficult to trace the actual events as they now unfold. The step-by-step accounts reported by Matthew and John appear slightly different. No doubt many more things transpired than we realize, and each of these men was reporting the scenes from a slightly different perspective, one drawing the details from one part of the events, the other from another part. But there are many things of which we can be sure.

He Speaks to Mary

Two women, both named Mary, were at the tomb about the time the angel came to roll the stone away. One of the Marys, Mary Magdalene, ran quickly and told the disciples what had happened. "They have taken the Lord out of the tomb," she said, "and we don't know where they have put him!" Peter and John immediately started running for the tomb. John outran Peter and arrived at the entrance. As he hesitated a moment before entering, Peter finally arrived and stepped inside. There before them lay strips of linen that had been wrapped about Jesus, as well as the burial cloth that had been around his head. But the disciples were confused as to the meaning of all this. They did not understand that Jesus must rise from the dead according to the Scripture. They departed for their homes.

Mary Magdalene, however, lingered a while longer. Weeping, she bent over to look into the tomb and saw two angels sitting where Jesus had been lying. "Woman, why are you crying?" they asked.

"They have taken my Lord away," she said, "and I don't know where they have put him."

We rejoice at the Passion of Christ but weep at the empty tomb. We seem to focus well on his suffering but somehow fail to realize how glorious is his Resurrection. How blind we are! When there is reason for concern we rejoice, and when we should be glad we are terrified.

Turning around, Mary saw Jesus standing before her but did not recognize him. When he asked why she was crying and what she was looking for, she assumed he was the gardener and answered, "Sir, if you have carried him away, tell me where you have put him, and I will get him."

Jesus said to her, "Mary."

"Teacher!" she cried.

After Jesus had spoken with her briefly, Mary returned to the disciples with the news, "I have seen the Lord."[2]

It wasn't seeing Jesus that convinced her it was truly him; it was his words to her. We believe, not because we have seen him but because he has called us by name. When Jesus said, "Mary," she suddenly became aware of the truth. Eternity began to focus clearly and she saw the Son of God. Had we stood beside her to behold the empty tomb, the angels, and the risen Lord, we too would have remained blinded until he called us by name.

Only by recognizing and responding to his call do we become free from comparing him with other men. We are no longer tempted to confuse God with Satan, good with evil, heaven with hell, success with failure, and life with death.

Jesus had just stepped beyond the grave. His Resurrection

was much different from that of the young man at Nain or of
Mary and Martha's brother, Lazarus. Though life had reen-
tered their lifeless bodies, they remained subject to death.
That bondage had not been removed. But when Christ came
forth, he was transformed. He had conquered death so that it
no longer had a hold on him.

If we are to understand the mystery of death, we must
begin by understanding that death does not mean "nonexist-
ence." It means "separation from intended purpose." When
Christ was separated from his body, it was only temporary.
Hell could not hold him. Hell can hold only sin and rebellion.
Jesus took our sins there, but he was able to escape because
there is only righteousness in him.

He Speaks to Two Disciples on the Road to Emmaus

Two disciples, unable to figure out what had happened,
had pretty much given up hope in Jesus. Initially they believed he was the long-awaited Messiah, but their own rea-
soning now confused them.

Walking the road to Emmaus, Jesus met them but they did
not recognize him. As they walked, they carefully explained
to this "stranger" all that had happened recently in Jerusalem.
Jesus, however, responded by rebuking them. "How foolish
you are, and how slow of heart to believe all that the prophets
have spoken!"[3]

Jesus did not rebuke the disciples because they did not
understand what was happening or failed to recognize him but
because they did not believe the Scriptures.

Jesus was intent on pointing them to the Word of God:
"And beginning with Moses and all the Prophets, he explained to them what was said in all the Scriptures concerning

himself."[4] He carefully showed them that the entire Old Testament exists to point men to himself. When the veil is removed, it reveals the glory of the Son. The Old Testament speaks concerning the sinner and the disgrace that has befallen him, but it also quickly points to the promised redemption which is in Jesus. Despite all Jesus had said to these disciples, they still did not perceive that it was he. It was not until later, while dining with him in a nearby village, that, as he broke bread and gave it to them, their eyes were opened. Immediately he disappeared from their sight.

The revelation of Jesus and the revelation of Scripture are one and the same. Luke uses the same word to describe the opening of their eyes to recognize Jesus that he uses to describe the opening of their minds so they could understand the Scriptures. The Old Testament Scriptures remain closed to all but those who have, by faith, accepted the resurrected Lord.

He Appears to the Disciples

Later, as the disciples gathered in a locked room because they feared the Jews, Jesus came and stood in their midst. He showed them his hands and side. And so it would be forever established that he was not an apparition, he said, "Touch me and see; a ghost does not have flesh and bones, as you see I have."[5]

The very same body that hung on the cross now stood before them—but it was a body that had been changed remarkably, having put on immortality. His appearance was sudden, as if out of nowhere. Later he would ascend to the Father just as mysteriously.

He Speaks to Thomas

Thomas, one of the Twelve, was not present when these things happened. When told of them he doubted, saying,

"Unless I see the nail marks in his hands and put my finger where the nails were, and put my hand into his side, I will not believe it."[6]

Thomas's problem was more than doubt; it was the sin of unbelief. Thomas was no longer seeking God. His words were not *when I see*, as if to indicate he was still looking. They were *unless I see*. His skepticism bore the marks of rebellion. He demanded proof by the method fallen man always uses: his senses. "Unless I see, unless I touch." He had been told by faithful friends that Christ was alive but insisted on holding on to his stubbornness. Such arrogance demands nothing but the wrath of God. But in Jesus this blasphemer found the love of God.

A week later when the disciples, including Thomas, had gathered together again, Jesus suddenly stood in their midst. He encouraged Thomas to examine his wounds so he would stop doubting and believe. In the face of stubbornness and rebellion, insult and arrogance, Jesus loved the sin right out of this man of unbelief. How could God submit to such irreverence? Only God himself could contain such compassion. In amazement, Thomas declared, "My Lord and my God." He stood face-to-face with the risen Lord and called him God. He acknowledged that before him stood the one true God. In a moment, Thomas was changed completely by the love of God, never to be the same again.

Although Jesus submitted to Thomas's need to see, he told him, "Because you have seen me, you have believed; blessed are those who have not seen and yet have believed."[7] Those who were yet to come to know Christ, who would not see and yet would believe, were to be blessed because of their faith.

He Speaks to the Disciples by the Seashore

Later, Jesus appeared to his disciples along the shores of the Sea of Tiberias. Peter, Thomas, Nathanael, James and

John—the two sons of Zebedee, and two other disciples had gone fishing. They had fished all night but had caught nothing. In the morning Jesus stood on the shore and called to them, "Friends, haven't you any fish?" Not realizing who he was, they answered no. "Throw your net on the right side of the boat and you will find some," Jesus responded. Doing so, they found they were unable to draw in the net because of the large number of fish. Then John said, "It is the Lord." Peter immediately wrapped his outer garment about him and jumped into the water as the other disciples began following in the boat with the netful of fish in tow. Reaching shore, they found Jesus with bread and fish roasting on a fire. He said, "Bring some of the fish you have just caught." The net contained 153 fish. "Come," he said, "and have breakfast."[8]

He Speaks to Peter

"When they had finished eating, Jesus said to Simon Peter, 'Simon son of John, do you truly love me more than these?'
" 'Yes, Lord,' he said, 'you know that I love you.' "[9]
What was in Jesus' words? Was he testing Peter to see if he would deny him? Was this a subtle rebuke for his sin of the past? Probably not.

Peter's former sin had been settled. Jesus was not digging up the past, but perhaps he was making sure Satan would not dig it up either. Three times Jesus asked the question, "Do you love me?" and three times Jesus exhorted, "Feed my sheep."[10] Forever Peter would remember his recommission into service. He would never have to question the love, mercy, and grace bestowed upon him at that moment.

Great love generates great love. Peter's eventual prominence probably lay in the fact that he was able to bestow on others the same compassion that had been bestowed upon him. He loved much because he had been forgiven much.

Jesus had made it clear that the sheep were his and not Peter's. Augustine noted the commission as, "Feed My sheep as Mine, not as yours; seek My glory in them, not yours; My kingdom, not yours; My wealth, not yours."

Peter had been asked to become a shepherd but was still a lamb. Jesus had become a Lamb but was still the Shepherd.

Jesus Commissions His Disciples

"He said to them, 'Go into all the world and preach the good news to all creation. Whoever believes and is baptized will be saved, but whoever does not believe will be condemned.' "[11] What did the Father send the Son to do? He was to invade darkness with light. What does the Son send us to do? The same thing! As the Son operated in total obedience to the Father, so we are to operate in obedience to the Son.

Jesus was God in the flesh, but he never used his deity in overcoming. He received power from the Holy Spirit through anointing. We are to receive the same power. "And with that he breathed on them and said, 'Receive the Holy Spirit.' "[12] This was not the first time he sent them out. He had sent them out before the cross at a time they understood very little about the kingdom of God, and in their ignorance were tempted to do the work of God in their own strength. Now, however, they were ready to receive help from God.

Prayer became important to the early Church, not as a means of getting things from God but as a means of learning to work more closely with him. Prayer does not make us better people by making us stronger in our abilities.

Prayer changes us into different people. It makes loving people out of those who are full of hatred and turns sinners into saints. It turns discouragement into courage, weakness into strength, arrogance into humility, sadness into joy, and turmoil into peace.

After Jesus said, "Receive the Holy Spirit," he went on to say, "If you forgive anyone his sins, they are forgiven; if you do not forgive them, they are not forgiven."[13] Christ did not give the disciples power to forgive sins as if they had borne them as he had. He is the only one who can forgive sins directly, but indirectly and as his representatives, he gave the disciples the authority to forgive. As the Father had sent him, he was sending them. That means that in the same manner and with the same authority the Father had commissioned him, he was commissioning his followers. The closeness of communion by prayer and the infilling of the Holy Spirit would keep them from arbitrary and capricious acts outside of the will of God. They were not to make independent judgments according to their whims and fancies. They were to carry out the will of God according to the Word of God. Thus, when they spoke, it was as if the Son himself were speaking. The messenger of Christ was in effect a "little Christ" and in that capacity became known as a Christian.

Their message would bring life and hope to those who believed and death and despair to those who did not believe. The one who repented received forgiveness. The one who did not was condemned. But this was not the judgment of the disciples. It was the effect of the Word which they preached.

What great responsibility was given to these men who had already proven themselves untrustworthy! But their weakness was strengthened as they were borne aloft by the "all power" of heaven now given to them.

Was the authority given for preaching and teaching and even for doing miracles to be available to all believers, or was it simply the spark that was to set the early Church aflame? Jesus made no distinction but said, "I tell you the truth, *anyone* who has faith in me will do what I have been doing. He will do even greater things than these, because I am going to the Father" (italics added).[14]

Edmund Schlink wrote, "Neither fear of the unusual nor recognition of personal weakness of faith should keep the congregation of today from reckoning with signs and wonders. At no time should the Church of Jesus Christ be without those who in faith dare lay their hands upon the sick for healing and dare command devils to come out of those who are possessed."[15]

And let us not be unbelieving as Thomas. If we do not see healings and Satan continues to harass, we still must be obedient. If one lives but another dies, we must not become faithless.

Schlink went on to say, "What are we to think when Peter's hands were stretched out on the arm of the cross and he died, while, according to an ancient legend, the poison that was given John to drink did not harm him? The risen Christ replies: 'If I will that he tarry till I come, what is that to thee?' " (John 21:22).[16]

"You must follow me."[17]

Notice the words of Paul Rees:

Thus the fact of Jesus' death became completely counterbalanced by another fact—the fact of his resurrection. It was this fact, plus the giving of the Holy Spirit, that turned that group of whipped and broken men into a closely-knit fellowship of flaming crusaders who gave the initial push to the most redemptive movement ever launched among men—the Christian Church. Those men caught the Easter message—Christ crucified and risen from the dead—and they insisted, as they passed the torch along, that it was the message of a crowning fact.[18]

☙12☙
Victory in Jesus

The Resurrection of Jesus Christ provides the greatest hope mankind has ever known. With it we are guaranteed life after death, a home in heaven, and a new body to replace the one defiled by sin. Such a hope has a drastic effect upon our approach to the life we now live in the flesh. Because of his Resurrection, we are able to walk in confidence, assurance, faith, and love, unburdened by guilt and condemnation.

Justification: Putting the Past in Order

The most wonderful aspect of God's love for us is found in his willingness to pay the price for our sin. He asks only that we accept and follow his Son. The just Judge now has become the Justifier. The past is gone under the blood of Christ. All penalties have been paid.

With Christ living within us, we now have the proper motivation for doing what is right. Christ is not only the pattern for righteousness, he is also the *power* for righteousness.

God does not expect a person to obtain goodness without his help.

Sanctification: Keeping the Present in Order

We might call justification "grace without works." It happens without an ounce of energy on our part. Sanctification, on the other hand, could be referred to as "working grace."

Such wonderful sanctification can be hindered in many ways. The practice of sin is one of them. Another is to focus attention on the lives of other people rather than on Christ. Whether it is a shrimp of a man who by his sinfulness angers us, or a giant of a man who by his faithfulness intimidates us, we will always be discouraged by the discomforting shape of the human profile.

God never meant that sanctification would separate us totally from the physical world. True, we are to be set apart unto him, but his intent was that we would no longer participate in the world's system, not be taken out of or away from the physical world or its people.

Participation is a key word to understanding sanctification. Many have believed that *association* was the key word, but this is not necessarily so. The Scripture tells us not to associate with unrepentant people who call themselves brothers but who practice sin. But we are free to associate with the unbeliever as long as we are not participating in or sanctioning his sin. When the life of Christ fills every part of our being we can venture forth, without fear, to where there are people with needs. Purity of mind and heart are best assured when we have a dynamic relationship with the One who lives within us, and when we are endeavoring to allow him to love others through us.

Authority in Christ

The Gospel message is one of power and authority. In the words of Paul Rees:

> That is the message of Easter! Power, through this risen Savior, to break the spell of wrong thinking in your life and mine: power to snap the fetters of unworthy habits: power to cancel out the guilt of long-standing sins: power to take weak and defeated Christians and turn them into living embodiments of the beauty of holiness: power to uproot and destroy bad tempers and wrong attitudes and in their place set the white flowers of Christlikeness: power to make the humblest among us a channel of blessing, an instrument of benediction, to the distraught world in which we live: power—blessed be God!—to carry them through the stern realities of life, across the turbid waters of death's dark river and to plant their feet, tired but triumphant, in the Paradise of God.[1]

Two important Scriptures point us to the kind of authority and power Jesus used when he was here on earth and the kind manifested in the Book of Acts. "I tell you the truth," Jesus said, "anyone who has faith in me will do what I have been doing. He will do even greater things than these, because I am going to the Father."[2] To this great promise we add the words of Jesus as recorded in the Gospel of Luke: "I have given you authority to trample on snakes and scorpions and to overcome all the power of the enemy; nothing will harm you."[3]

The major question concerns what Jesus was doing and what we are to do with the authority he has handed to us.

John tells us that the reason Jesus appeared was to destroy the works of the devil. Christ showed this as throughout his ministry he dealt with demon spirits, casting them out and healing people oppressed by them. Some would suppose that these were isolated instances, but Scripture shows us that the extent of the Enemy's work reaches into every area of human existence. John talked about the "whole world" being under the "control of the evil one."[4]

Jesus came to deal with the devil and left us the power to continue what he started. That means we have not only the right but the ability to cast out demons, heal the sick, and raise the dead. Jesus did these things. And remember his words: "Anyone who has faith in me will do what I have been doing."

Where would a person begin who desired to be used of the Lord in such a manner? Initially, we must realize that it is impossible to do anything on our own. Jesus said, "I am the vine; you are the branches. If a man remains in me and I in him, he will bear much fruit; *apart from me you can do nothing.*"[5] The psalmist noted, "Unless the Lord builds the house, its builders labor in vain."[6]

It is easy to look at a troubled world and be tempted to do some great work on our own. Many Christians look at rest homes, jail cells, and even hospitals for the mentally ill and want to march in and take over for Jesus. Those who have tried without God's direction have met with failure. Why, then, the provision for power but what seems to be its limited working?

The answer lies in knowing the heart of God. We cannot see behind the scenes to know why people are the way they are. Some have been tricked by the Enemy; others have given in to him freely. Some want deliverance, others do not. Some are bound by weak spirits, others by "strongmen." And some just plain enjoy sinning without caring about the consequences. To try to walk in the arena of deliverance without God's careful guidance is foolishness. But to walk there in his anointing is miraculous.

God's provision for working directly with us is his Holy Spirit. While Jesus was here on earth, he told of the coming of the Spirit to lead and to guide us: "But when he, the Spirit of truth, comes," Jesus said, "he will guide you into all truth."[7] He also said, "But you will receive power when the Holy Spirit comes on you; and you will be my witnesses in Jerusalem, and in all Judea and Samaria, and to the ends of the earth."[8]

New birth in Christ results in a changed nature. Where once we were controlled by the evil Enemy, we now become the temple of the Holy Spirit. Although we cannot have a devil in us, we can have demons affecting us. The devil cannot indwell our spirit, but demons can affect our soul. Demons may attack our minds incessantly to keep the human spirit from being at the control center of our lives. But because of Christ we have the ability to keep from being overcome. Since he has come to take up residence from within, we now have power to "take captive every thought to make it obedient to Christ."[9]

The inner working of the Holy Spirit gives us the strength needed to resist Satan's attacks. That power in us frees us from bondage and allows us to help others to freedom as well. And though we still live in a body of flesh, we are free from being forced into sin because our new nature makes us dead to sin. We are no longer compelled to serve either the Enemy or our own bodies. Should we do so, it is only because we have made that choice.

Through the Holy Spirit, we are able to resist evil spirits. However, because the Enemy has been around a lot longer than we have and because he has superior knowledge and understanding, he is able to prevent us from hindering him on our own. But with God's leading and authority, we find all we need for effective warfare against the demonic realm. And the best place to begin is in intercessory prayer.

The Basis of Our Authority

On the Isle of Patmos, John wrote, "Now have come the salvation and the power and the kingdom of our God, and the authority of his Christ. For the accuser of our brothers, who accuses them before our God day and night, has been hurled down. *They overcame him by the blood of the Lamb and by the word of their testimony;* they did not love their lives so much as to shrink from death."[10]

Much has been said about blood. We have seen that God signed a blood covenant with us and he paid the price for our failure to keep the covenant by the shedding of his own blood. But how are we to look at the blood of the Lamb so that it might be made powerful to us in putting down Satan?

First, we realize daily that we can approach God with confidence because of the blood. Nothing has a right to hinder our fellowship with him. We can come and rejoice in his presence as often as we want. The devil can't stop a child of God from entering the throne room because he is in covenant relationship with God.

Next, when demons come to harass, we can command them to leave because they have no authority over a blood-washed saint. Often our spoken knowledge of the power of the blood of Jesus is sufficient to cause them to retreat.

Victory in Christ

Do you realize that in right relationship with Jesus Christ you have authority to resist both the flesh and the devil, as well as power to stand against the world? Are you appropriating that power, or has the Enemy deceived you into believing that such is only for "special" people? One of Satan's basic schemes is to belittle you so much that you will not rise in Jesus to work against him (Satan). Put a halt to Satan's work today by confessing to the Lord every aspect of the state you are in. His grace is sufficient to cleanse every sin. You *are* victorious in Christ.

❧ 13 ❧
The Eternal Life of Jesus Christ

Jesus Christ Is Eternal Life

Eternal life is not "living forever," although living forever is a part of eternal life. Eternal life is the Person of God. It is the very life of God, found in the Father, the Son, and the Holy Spirit. "The life appeared; we have seen it and testify to it, and *we proclaim to you the eternal life, which was with the Father and has appeared to us.*"[1] Before his arrest and crucifixion, as Jesus taught the disciples he looked toward heaven and prayed, "Father, the time has come. Glorify your Son, that your Son may glorify you. For you granted him authority over all people that he might give eternal life to all those you have given him. *Now this is eternal life: that they may know you, the only true God, and Jesus Christ, whom you have sent.*"[2]

To Know Him

Like some unseen magnetic pull, men and women are drawn to the Savior. Even the rebellious often feel the tug.

They sense the life they are missing, which suggests that nothing else will fulfill their needs like his presence.

The Apostle Paul wrote to the Philippians that he wanted to really "know" God. His words reveal a heart that cries for closeness with God. They are words of spiritual desperation.

Paul doesn't speak these words because Jesus has campaigned loudly to attract people. When Christ calls he calls tenderly, almost silently. When we are hungry for his presence we move without so much as a thought, like swallows carried on the wind, migrating to a far-off land.

Or, if he were to walk by, with hardly a glance he would cause men and women who long for righteousness to lay down their tools and follow. Something unique and wonderful about him reaches the deepest part of our being.

When Jesus does speak, his words are authoritative and we look to him for leadership. His confidence inspires new faith. A genuine concern for others brings admiration. When he is there, we do not question that it is him. But when he seems far away, we wonder where he has gone and are sometimes tempted to follow another.

Without complete dedication to him, we might become careless in our devotion when his nearness is not felt. Should we look away even momentarily, he becomes difficult to see and easy to misunderstand, especially when other interests so quickly occupy our attention. And only men and women whose hearts long for righteousness will ever truly see and really get to know him.

When Joan of Arc set about to deliver her country, she was invited to the king's court. But his majesty had disguised himself in the dress of a courier and placed the courier on his throne. For some unknown reason, Joan of Arc passed by the person on the throne and bowed before the king in courier's dress. She had never seen him before but recognized him regardless. So it is with the man or woman who has set his heart to know no other but the King of kings.

To Love Him

That the very God of creation is offering a relationship of mutual concern and love is beyond comprehension. That God would reveal himself to humanity and then offer to fellowship with us becomes difficult for our fallen nature to accept.

The declaration that "God so loved the world" does not easily translate into "God loves me." But God does love us, even when we find it hard to believe. Usually it is our own sin that makes his love seem foreign. His love is there if we care to establish a relationship with him through Jesus.

Loving God is the result of receiving his love. "This is love: not that we loved God, but that he loved us and sent his Son as an atoning sacrifice for our sins."[3]

14

Companions in Eternity

A Bride for the Son

Facing life is much easier if we believe that behind it all there is an ultimate purpose. Regardless of the pain, the suffering, the sorrow, and the disappointments of life, we find strength if we can believe our trouble is not in vain.

But what really is the reason for all our problems? What is the purpose behind this strange existence of ours? Finding the answers to these questions changes the way we look at life as well as the way we handle it.

What is God after? What is he trying to accomplish? Surprisingly, his Word gives a very simple answer. *He wants a Bride for his Son.* All of life as we know it, all of history—past, present, and future—exists for one reason: to provide an Eternal Companion for the Son of God, a Bride,[1] a Wife for the Lamb.

In order to fulfill his plan God began to create, and a vast

and beautiful universe came into existence. He created the
earth. It was to be the place where he would place his prized
possession. He created the sun and eventually millions of
other suns, planets, and moons. Finally God made mankind,
an entity in his own image and likeness. And he made this
unique creation for divine fellowship.

But to truly have mankind love the Son without force or
fear, God would have to provide him free will. Only such a
plan would produce a being who would approach him in likeness and yet be subject to him. Free will would allow God to
draw his beloved into a relationship with himself. Unfortunately, it would also allow man to reject God's proposal.

Romance at the Heart of God

"For God so loved the world . . ." is still the "heart" of
God. In the depths of his being, he has purposed to bring
forth a Companion to love—his Bride. Hence, all that is happening is for that purpose.

God is after romance and not dictatorial rule, as the Enemy
would have us believe. The heart of God's Word is the herald
of the message of love. "This is love: not that we loved God,
but that he loved us and sent his Son as an atoning sacrifice for
our sins."[2] No suitor has ever given as much to prove his love
for the person of his affections.

Notice John makes it clear that the direction of love is first
God to man and not the other way around: "We love because
he first loved us."[3] Such all-encompassing love, should we
receive it by laying down our rebellion, will generate a response of "I love you too." John also makes it clear that as
individuals develop a love relationship with God, they will
love one another as well. "Dear friends, since God so loved
us, we also ought to love one another. No one has ever seen

God; but if we love one another, God lives in us and his love is made complete in us."[4]

History Working to Perfect the Bride

The Bride of Christ is to be pure and spotless. Christ "gave himself up for her to make her holy, cleansing her by the washing with water through the word, and to present her to himself as a radiant church, without stain or wrinkle or any other blemish, but holy and blameless."[5] As the Apostle Peter spoke of "looking forward to a new heaven and a new earth, the home of righteousness," he encouraged the saints by saying, "Dear friends, since you are looking forward to this, make every effort to be found spotless, blameless and at peace with him."[6] Paul wrote, "Do everything without complaining or arguing, so that you may become blameless and pure, children of God without fault."[7]

The perfection of the Bride is the responsibility of God himself. He will present her in accordance with his will. "For it is God who works in you to will and to act according to his good purpose."[8] Even the actual righteousness that is demanded is provided by him. Paul spoke of gaining Christ and being found in him, "not having a righteousness of my own that comes from the law, but that which is through faith in Christ—the righteousness that comes from God and is by faith."[9]

The struggles we now face are preparing us for future rulership with the Lord. Paul said to Timothy, "If we endure, we will also reign with him."[10] John recorded the words of Jesus: "To him who overcomes, I will give the right to sit with me on my throne."[11]

It is hard to imagine that anything good could come out of all the suffering on earth. But God's Word assures us that it will. All of the problems we presently face as Christians will one day show forth a now-hidden glory. "And we know that in all things God works for the good of those who love him [his Bride], who have been called according to his purpose [eternal rulership with him]."[12] "Now if we are children, then we are heirs—heirs of God and co-heirs with Christ, if indeed we share in his sufferings in order that we may also share in his glory. I consider that our present sufferings are not worth comparing with the glory that will be revealed in us."[13]

A Wedding

John, while in exile on the isle of Patmos, saw in a vision the culmination of all history. He wrote, "Then I heard what sounded like a great multitude, like the roar of rushing waters and like loud peals of thunder, shouting: 'Hallelujah! For our Lord God Almighty reigns. Let us rejoice and be glad and give him glory! For the wedding of the Lamb has come, and his bride has made herself ready. Fine linen, bright and clean, was given her to wear.' "[14]

In Conclusion

Soon the Bride and Groom will be united, and Christ and his Companion will rule the universe forever. This is the union God purposed from the beginning of time.

There has never been a greater story of love and romance. Now, as we wait for the promise of his coming, our heart yearns for him and we cry, "Come, Lord Jesus, come!"

References

Introduction

1. Philippians 1:6.
2. A. W. Tozer, *The Pursuit of God* (Harrisburg, Pennsylvania; Christian Publications, Inc., 1982), pp. 49, 50.

Chapter 1   The Birth of Jesus Christ

1. John MacBeath, *The Face of Christ* (London: Marshall Brothers Limited, n.d.), p. 13.
2. Romans 1:20.
3. Ibid.
4. C. S. Lewis, *Mere Christianity* (New York: Macmillan Publishing Company, 1943), p. 59.
5. Isaiah 7:14.
6. Matthew 1:23.
7. Luke 7:19.
8. Jeremiah 23:5, 6.

9. John 19:30.
10. Matthew 1:20, 21.
11. Hebrews 5:7 KJV.
12. Nehemiah 9:6.
13. John 5:17, 18.
14. Hebrews 1:3 (italics added).

Chapter 2 A New Birth for Mankind

1. John 3:7.
2. Ezekiel 36:25–27. *See also* Hebrews 10:16.
3. 2 Corinthians 5:17.
4. John 14:6.
5. Acts 4:12.
6. Romans 1:21.
7. John 3:19.
8. E. Y. Mullins, *Why Is Christianity True?* (Chicago: Christian Culture Press, 1905), pp. 294, 295.
9. Romans 6:14.
10. Revelation 3:20.

Chapter 3 The Growth of Jesus Christ

1. Luke 2:51.
2. John 12:49, 50.
3. Hebrews 5:8.
4. Hebrews 4:15.

Chapter 4 Christian Growth

1. John MacBeath, *The Face of Christ* (London: Marshall Brothers Limited, n.d.), p. 20.
2. 2 Corinthians 5:14.
3. Paul Rees, *The Radiant Cross* (Grand Rapids, Michigan: William B. Eerdmans Publishing Company, 1949), p. 20.
4. Quoted by Jesse Penn-Lewis in *The Story of Job* (Fort

Washington, Pennsylvania: The Overcomers Literature Trust, n.d.), p. 23.

5. 1 Peter 5:8.
6. 1 Peter 5:10.
7. 1 Peter 4:12, 13.
8. Romans 5:3, 4 (italics added).
9. 2 Corinthians 4:17 (italics added).
10. 2 Corinthians 1:3–5 (italics added).
11. John 16:33.
12. Jeremiah 12:5.
13. Exodus 1:12.
14. Rees, *Radiant Cross*, p. 26.

Chapter 5   The Ministry of Jesus Christ

1. Luke 1:42–45.
2. Luke 1:46–49.
3. Luke 3:3.
4. Mark 1:2, 3.
5. John 1:26, 27.
6. John 1:29–31.
7. John 1:32–34.
8. Luke 4:4.
9. Luke 4:6, 7.
10. Luke 4:8.
11. Luke 4:9–12.
12. Psalms 91:9–11.
13. John 12:31.
14. John 3:17.
15. Luke 12:51.
16. Matthew 4:23.

Chapter 6   Christian Ministry

1. John 13:34, 35.
2. 1 John 3:18.

3. Mark 12:30, 31.
4. 1 Corinthians 13:4–7.
5. Mark 10:43, 44.
6. 2 Timothy 2:15.
7. Psalms 133:1.
8. Galatians 5:21.
9. John 15:5.
10. Isaiah 1:23.

Chapter 7   Jesus in Gethsemane

1. Matthew 26:38.
2. Matthew 26:39.
3. Herschel H. Hobbs, *The Crucial Words From Calvary* (Grand Rapids: Baker Book House, 1959), p. 54.
4. Matthew 26:40, 41.
5. Matthew 26:42.
6. Matthew 26:51.
7. John 18:11.

Chapter 8   Gethsemane Experiences

1. Psalms 40:8 KJV.
2. Genesis 18:27.
3. Exodus 20:18, 19.
4. Galatians 6:17.

Chapter 9   Christ at Calvary

1. Exodus 24:7, 8.
2. Quoted by Jesse Penn-Lewis in *The Story of Job* (Fort Washington, Pennsylvania: The Overcomers Literature Trust, n.d.), p. 160.
3. Matthew 26:27, 28.
4. The ideas in this section, as in other parts of this book, are presented quite simplistically. The danger with this

simplification is that they may be misunderstood. The serious student, therefore, should resort to more extensive works for a more complete understanding.

5. 2 Corinthians 6:2.

6. Luke 19:10.

7. John R. W. Stott, *The Cross of Christ* (Downers Grove, Illinois: InterVarsity Press, 1986), p. 124.

8. Quoted by Myer Pearlman in *Knowing the Doctrines of the Bible* (Springfield, Missouri: Gospel Publishing House, 1937), p. 203.

9. Stott, *Cross,* p. 173.

10. Hebrews 10:4–10.

11. Hebrews 2:11.

12. 1 Corinthians 15:21.

13. A. W. Tozer, *Whatever Happened to Worship* (Camp Hill, Pennsylvania: Christian Publications, Inc., 1985), p. 11.

14. Hebrews 9:26.

15. John 19:19–22.

16. Revelation 13:8.

17. Philippians 2:9.

18. Luke 23:34.

19. John 19:24.

20. Luke 23:39–43.

21. Russell Bradley Jones, *Gold From Golgotha* (Grand Rapids: Baker Book House, 1959), p. 23. (Copyright 1945 by The Moody Bible Institute of Chicago.)

22. Luke 2:35.

23. Mark 3:33.

24. Edmund Schlink, *The Victor Speaks* (Saint Louis: Concordia Publishing House, 1958), p. 21.

25. John 19:26, 27.

26. Mark 15:34.

27. Philippians 2:6, 7.
28. 2 Corinthians 5:21.
29. John 19:28.
30. John 19:30.
31. Schlink, *Victor*, p. 80.
32. Herschel H. Hobbs, *The Crucial Words From Calvary* (Grand Rapids: Baker Book House, 1959), p. 96.

Chapter 10   Crucified With Christ

1. 1 Corinthians 2:2.
2. Oswald Chambers, *My Utmost for His Highest* (New York: Dodd, Mead & Company, 1935), p. 138.
3. 1 Peter 2:21.
4. 1 John 3:16.
5. Paul Rees, *The Radiant Cross* (Grand Rapids: William B. Eerdmans Publishing Company, 1949), p. 19.
6. D. L. Moody, *The Overcoming Life* (Old Tappan, New Jersey: Fleming H. Revell Company, 1896), p. 32.
7. Galatians 2:20.
8. Romans 6:6, 7.
9. Galatians 5:16 KJV.
10. Mark 8:34.
11. 2 Corinthians 12:10.
12. Quoted by Jesse Penn-Lewis in *The Story of Job* (Fort Washington, Pennsylvania: The Overcomers Literature Trust, n.d.).
13. Paul Billheimer, *Destined for the Cross* (Wheaton, Illinois: Tyndale House Publishers, Inc., 1982), p. 38.
14. Matthew 18:17.
15. Luke 13:3.
16. Acts 3:16.
17. Galatians 2:20.
18. Ephesians 3:12.

19. William Gurnall, *The Christian in Complete Armour* (Carlisle, Pennsylvania: The Banner of Trust, 1986), pp. 32, 33.

Chapter 11   The Resurrection of Jesus

1. Luke 24:21.
2. John 20:1–18.
3. Luke 24:25.
4. Luke 24:27.
5. Luke 24:39.
6. John 20:25.
7. John 20:29.
8. John 21:1–12.
9. John 21:15.
10. John 21:16.
11. Mark 16:15, 16.
12. John 20:22.
13. John 20:23.
14. John 14:12.
15. Edmund Schlink, *The Victor Speaks* (Saint Louis: Concordia Publishing House, 1958), p. 123.
16. Ibid., p. 124.
17. John 21:22.
18. Paul Rees, *The Radiant Cross* (Grand Rapids: William B. Eerdmans Publishing Company, 1949), p. 128.

Chapter 12   Victory in Jesus

1. Paul Rees, *The Radiant Cross* (Grand Rapids: William B. Eerdmans Publishing Company, 1949), pp. 133, 134.
2. John 14:12.
3. Luke 10:19.
4. 1 John 5:19.
5. John 15:5 (italics added).

6. Psalms 127:1.
7. John 16:13.
8. Acts 1:8.
9. 2 Corinthians 10:5.
10. Revelation 12:10, 11 (italics added).

Chapter 13   The Eternal Life of Jesus Christ

1. 1 John 1:2 (italics added).
2. John 17:1–3 (italics added).
3. 1 John 4:10.

Chapter 14   Companions in Eternity

1. The "Bride" of Christ as well as the "Wife" of Christ refer to the New Jerusalem, which comprises all the saints of all the ages and not just the Church.
2. 1 John 4:10.
3. 1 John 4:19.
4. 1 John 4:11, 12.
5. Ephesians 5:25–27.
6. 2 Peter 3:13, 14.
7. Philippians 2:14, 15.
8. Philippians 2:13.
9. Philippians 3:9.
10. 2 Timothy 2:12.
11. Revelation 3:21.
12. Romans 8:28.
13. Romans 8:17, 18.
14. Revelation 19:6–8.